THE
MAGICAL
USE OF
PRAYER
BEADS

About the Author

Jean-Louis de Biasi is a author, lecturer, and Hermetic philosopher who has studied the various topics of the tradition since
the 1970s, and who has been initiated into the highest degrees
of several Western initiatic traditions. Introduced very early
into the Ordo Aurum Solis, in 2003 de Biasi became the tenth
Lifetime Grand Master. He is also in charge as Reverend of the
religious expression of the Hermetic tradition called Ecclesia
Ogdoadica.

De Biasi's philosophical and spiritual tradition is rooted in
Neoplatonic and Hermetic affiliations, and includes masters
of the tradition such as Plato, Proclus, Iamblicus, the Emperor
Julian, Pletho, and Ficino, to name a few. He is also the Grand
Patriarch in charge of the Ordre Kabbalistique de la Rose-Croix
(the Kabbalistic Order of the Rose-Cross, O.K.R.C.).

He was initiated into Freemasonry and raised in 1992. He
is a 32° Scottish Rite Freemason, Southern Jurisdiction, U.S.,

F.G.C.R., Royal Arch Mason. He is a specialist of Masonic Rituals and Esoteric Freemasonry.

He is invited regularly to various countries where he gives workshops, seminars, trainings, and conferences on philosophical and traditional subjects and expounds on his writings.

He is the author of several books in French, which have been translated into several languages, and he is now writing in English for Llewellyn Publications.

To read more about Jean-Louis de Biasi, please visit him online:

https://www.facebook.com/jeanlouis.debiasi
http://www.debiasi.org
http://www.aurumsolis.info

Jean-Louis de Biasi

THE

MAGICAL
USE OF
PRAYER

BEADS

SECRET
Meditations & Rituals
for Your
Qabalistic, Hermetic,
Wiccan or Druid Practice

Llewellyn Publications
Woodbury, Minnesota

FIRST EDITION
First Printing, 2016

Cover image: iStockphoto.com/19973242/©burakpekakcan
Cover design: Lisa Novak

Llewellyn Publications is a registered trademark of Llewellyn Worldwide Ltd.

Library of Congress Cataloging-in-Publication Data
Names: Biasi, Jean-Louis de, author.
Title: The Magical Use of Prayer Beads : secret Meditations and Rituals for Your Qabalistic, Hermetic, Wiccan, or Druid Practice / Jean-Louis de Biasi.
Description: First Edition. | Woodbury, Minnesota : Llewellyn Publications, 2016.
Identifiers: LCCN 2016000964 (print) | LCCN 2016002058 (ebook) | ISBN 9780738747293 | ISBN 9780738748535 ()
Subjects: LCSH: Beads—Religious aspects. | Prayer.
Classification: LCC BL619.B43 B53 2016 (print) | LCC BL619.B43 (ebook) | DDC 203/.7—dc23

Llewellyn Publications
A Division of Llewellyn Worldwide Ltd.
2143 Wooddale Drive
Woodbury, MN 55125.2989
www.llewellyn.com

Printed in the United States of America

To my grandmother Monica de Biasi (Spadetto),
born in the city of Mosnigo, Italy, who unveiled
some of the Mysteries of the prayer beads for me.
(1898–1983)

Acknowledgments

This book is special to me on several levels. For a few years, I was lucky to have Donald Michael Kraig, a famous figure of the magick community, as editor. We exchanged hundreds of emails, talking about my writings. This book has been discussed with him, as have several forthcoming books you will progressively discover. Don gave his expertise to several chapters and commented on a few chapters before he died too young from cancer. It was his last work on a book in his life. I want to offer again my deep gratitude to him—for his advice, for the time spent to comment on and discuss the rituals and theory developed in my books. His invaluable understanding of spirituality and the occult world will always be remembered.

I would also like to offer my grateful thanks to Bruce Mac-Lennan for his foreword. His knowledge and understanding of the Western tradition is well-known and I highly recommend the reading of his book *The Wisdom of Hypatia*.

I would also like to thank Larry Phillips and Brian Morrow for their expertise and help with various parts of this book.

Finally, I want to thank the initiates of the Aurum Solis working in several countries with ancient rituals. They had the chance to experiment with a few of these rituals and their feedback was (and still is) always useful.

Contents

Foreword . . . xv

Introduction . . . 1

Chapter 1: **What Are Prayer Beads? . . . 5**

Chapter 2: **Main Principles for a Successful Practice . . . 13**

Chapter 3: **Consecration of Your Prayer Beads . . . 29**

Chapter 4: **Qabalistic Tradition . . . 43**
    Ritual of the Blazing Wheel   44
    Ritual of the 22 Keys   61
    Ritual of the Tree of Life   71
    Ritual of the Nine Choirs of Angels   78

Chapter 5: **Hermetic Tradition . . . 105**
    Ritual of the Circled Cross   106
    Ritual of the Seven Spheres   125
    Ritual of the Spiritual Ladder   140
    Ritual of the Hermetic Palindrome   154

Chapter 6: **Wiccan Tradition . . . 167**
    Ritual of the Wheel of the Year   168
    Ritual of the Goddess   196
    Ritual of the God   210

Chapter 7: **Druid Tradition . . . 231**
    Ritual of the Tribann   235
    Ritual of the Celtic Cross   255
    Ritual of the Nemeton   273

Conclusion . . . 297

Appendix . . . 299

    Guidelines for Greek Pronunciation   299

    Guidelines for Hebrew Pronunciation   303

Foreword

We have made beads for a very long time. The oldest discovered so far are Middle Stone Age pierced shells that date back 82,000 years.[1] They were transported more than 25 miles, some as far as 125 miles, inland from the North African shore where they were collected. These were no doubt precious possessions of the spiritual and temporal leaders of their communities, and are considered some of the earliest indicators of human symbolic activity.

What did our ancestors do with their beads? We cannot know, but we can make some reasonable guesses. No doubt they fingered them in moments of idleness, when worried, or when contemplating an issue, as people do now with their worry beads (Greek, *komboloi*). The preciousness of the beads would reinforce the insights arising from a meditative state of mind and lead to the beads being understood as spiritual tools. And this

---

1. Abdeljalil Bouzouggar, Nick Barton, et al., "82,000-year-old shell beads from North Africa and implications for the origins of modern human behavior," *Proceedings of the National Academy of Sciences USA*, 104 (2007), 9964–9969.

is how prayer beads have been used, from Hindu *malas* in the eighth century BCE to prayer beads of all sorts in the present day.

Neoplatonic philosophy and Theurgy (which are the heart of the Western esoteric traditions) provide a framework for understanding how prayer beads work as spiritual instruments. According to Neoplatonic cosmology, as found in Plotinus, Proclus, Iamblichus, and others, the cosmos is an emanation of The Ineffable One, the ultimate principle of unity, through several levels of reality. One of these is the Cosmic Mind (*Noûs*, in Greek), which is the realm of the changeless Platonic Ideas and the eternal gods. Below this is the Cosmic Soul, which animates the entire universe and unifies it as a single living organism. It governs the Cosmic Body, that is, the material world, which we experience through our senses. Therefore everything in the world exists in lineages or lines of descent from the gods and ultimately from The One. As a consequence, objects, properties, actions, and other things in the material world function as symbols (Grk., *symbola*) and tokens (Grk., *synthêmata*) that can be used to draw down these divine powers. More correctly, as Iamblichus explains, when used in ritual they tune our souls so that our souls resonate with specific divine energies and draw us up to the gods.

Prayer beads therefore are tools of *Theurgy* (Grk., "god-work"), the use of ritual to bring us into communion with the gods. The more symbols and tokens that are used, the closer this communion will be (other things being equal). Therefore, in constructing or selecting prayer beads, we must choose symbols that correspond with the divine powers we intend to invoke. As explained by Grand Master Jean-Louis de

Biasi, this includes the number of beads, their arrangement (e.g., division into groups), their material, their color, their shape, and all other aspects of their construction. Forgo no opportunity to strengthen the divine bond by means of correspondences.

Prayer beads are most often strung in a loop, which has great significance, for then the beads become a *mandala*, a symbol of the cosmos in its balance, unity, and wholeness. The string symbolizes the hidden inner bond that ties the disparate parts together, which gives unity to apparent multiplicity. For example, the beads may be divided into four groups representing the quarters (North, East, South, West) and other things corresponding to them, such as the four elements. However, a loop of prayer beads especially symbolizes cyclic time, such as the cycle of the year, the zodiac, the days of the week, and the phases of the moon. These lead to other correspondences, such as the Twelve Olympian Gods, the Seven Planets, and the Triple Goddess. Construct your prayer beads according to your spiritual goal.

Of course, after you string the beads, you have to tie the ends together in some way to make a loop. This is a magical binding operation and closes the circuit, so to speak, of the cycle and confines the energy in it. You can do this carefully, hiding the join if your intent is to symbolize a cycle with no beginning and no end. But often we want to connect with cycles that have a special place in them, and so the ends are joined in a conspicuous way and bound into a "Head" with a linear string of one or more beads and a tassel. This too has important significance. For, as Aristotle explained, the circle represents the unending motion of the heavens, but the straight line represents change occurring in the material world, which begins and ends: the mortality of life on earth. In Greek prayer beads, the Head is called the Priest; in Hindu tradition it is the Guru bead. Therefore, the Head indicates a special point of entry into the cycle and of exit from it, a liminal place of contact with the divine.

Neoplatonic philosophy teaches that each level of reality obeys a *triadic principle*, by which it *abides* in itself, *proceeds* downward to create lower levels, which then *return* upward seeking order and harmony. We enact this principle in time when we pray the beads, starting with the Head, which remains in its place, and praying around the cycle, away from the Head but then back to it, over and over, in imitation of the endless cycle of procession and return. While praying we contemplate this circle that binds the levels of the cosmos into one. Each time we pass the Head, we contemplate The One, which binds the cosmos into a unity.

The beads also symbolize the human life cycle, starting with our descent from the divine realms, symbolized by the Priest; proceeding into greater material manifestation; and then, as we pass the midpoint of life, a turn back towards the spiritual realms as we prepare to abandon the material world and return to the divine. Each time around the circle of beads is an opportunity to contemplate your life as a whole—what has passed and what is yet to come.

On a smaller scale, the loop symbolizes a single year with each bead representing a day (even if there are less than 365 of them). As you inhale and exhale on each bead, treat it as a new day, perfect in itself, without regret or nostalgia for those passed, and without worry or hope for those to come. The

Priest/Guru bead represents a significant anniversary, such as your birthday or your date of initiation (your rebirth). Candidates for initiation may string their own prayer beads, but the teacher and initiate together tie the final knots—the binding—and consecrate the completed beads. Candidates receive their completed beads when they are initiated.

"Like knows like" is an ancient philosophical principle, which implies that to know the gods, you must become like them: that is, tranquil, impassive, stable, and consistent in character. Moreover, to know The Ineffable One, you must become like it: that is, completely simple, unified, and unchanging. You can approach this state by meditating on something simple, such as your breath. The prayer beads help you to time your meditation, and each new bead reminds you to return your attention to your breath, in case it has wandered. To connect with a specific divine energy, you can repeat—in your mind or out loud—an appropriate prayer or mantra. Especially useful are very short "arrow prayers," so called because they shoot your soul directly into the heart of divinity. (For more on arrow prayers, see my book *The Wisdom of Hypatia*, Chapter 11.)

Although it might seem redundant in the face of 82,000 years of practical experience, contemporary psychotherapy also supports the spiritual benefits of prayer beads.[2] In one respect, this is not surprising, since some psychotherapeutic techniques are direct descendants of ancient spiritual practices. An effective modern technique, *cognitive behavioral therapy*, which is based on reframing your evaluation of events, is derived directly from ancient Stoicism (the Second Degree in *The Wisdom*

---

2. Uri Wernik, "The use of prayer beads in psychotherapy," *Mental Health, Religion & Culture*, 12 (2009), 359–368.

of Hypatia). Techniques such as *active imagination* in Jung's analytic psychology descend from Neoplatonic Theurgy (the Third Degree). All the many contemporary techniques of positive thinking arose in the New Thought movement of the early twentieth century, which was an outgrowth of American Trancendentalism, which was developed by Ralph Waldo Emerson and other thinkers influenced by Neoplatonism and Eastern wisdom traditions.

Dion Fortune defined magic as the art of changing consciousness at will, and prayer beads are important magical tools for transforming consciousness. Psychologically, simple positive thinking may be ineffective, and what is required is a more explicit reconstruction of the narrative, that is, a reframing of some personal story so that it has a better outcome. To accomplish this, you can choose individual beads to represent specific ideas (e.g., people, objects, events, affirmations), and string them together to construct a narrative that transforms negative thoughts into positive thoughts. Obviously, you should think carefully about the symbolism of your beads, perhaps with the assistance of your spiritual teacher. This book will give you much good advice.

You can make your prayer beads by yourself or with the help of your spiritual teacher, who may have better insights than you do into your situation and how it can be improved. Making the prayer beads can be a fun and creative activity, which already begins the transformation to a more positive state. Make it a ritual, but a constructive, positive, joyous ritual.

If you wear your prayer beads or carry them with you, they function as a talisman, constantly reinforcing the psychical transformation they are bringing about. However, they are most effective when you use them in ritual, for as you pull each bead through your fingers, saying or thinking what it means, you are reinforcing the sequence of ideas that you have constructed, taking your mind through a sequence of states and imprinting a pattern on it. If you speak your prayers out loud as you pull the beads, then thought, word, and action are united. If you also look at the colors and shapes of beads, then vision is engaged, in addition to hearing and touch. The calm and regular movement is relaxing and can induce a suggestible, hypnotic state. All these aid the transformation of your psyche. Praying the beads turns abstract thoughts into reality; it is a *spell*.

Prayer beads are simple yet powerful tools for self-transformation, proved through thousands of years of use in many spiritual traditions. *The Magical Use of Prayer Beads* will teach you how to use them to bring about your own spiritual transformation.

Bruce J. MacLennan

Introduction

Prayer beads can be found all around the world and were used thousands of years ago in various contexts. The goal of this book is not to write a history of prayer beads or to provide another guide for handcrafted jewelry. It is to give you a clear, fast, and efficient initiation into their use. This wonderful object is an amazing help that can transform the way you pray, meditate, or perform rituals.

When I was a child, all the Catholic women were using prayer beads in their devotion. Years later, in all my travels in Greece and throughout the Middle East I saw prayer beads being used constantly in daily life. By contrast, modern spiritual groups are not using this helpful tool, missing an opportunity to facilitate the inner work.

It is time to unveil the mysteries of prayer beads in a traditional way. Just a few minutes will be enough to understand the powerful combination that exists between symbols, sacred words, and visualizations.

The only thing you will need to activate the hidden power of these rituals in your life will be a few beads, a deep breath, and this book.

Welcome to the magical chain!

How to Use This Book

This book is intended to be a practical guide to the use of prayer beads. For this reason, it has been precisely organized.

For the first time in the history of the Western tradition, you are about to discover a very efficient and magical tool: prayer beads.

Knowing that such a magical tool exists is good, but holding a handbook that provides descriptions of the various prayer beads, meditations, and rituals from four Western traditions is much better!

What You Can Do with This Book

1. Understand what prayer beads are and their uses.

2. Know what the main principles of the rituals and practices are: energies, egregore, mantras, visualizations, etc.

3. Learn the way to bless and consecrate these tools.

4. A clear presentation of four different Western traditions.

5. For each of these traditions, discover symbols, descriptions, and practices involving various prayer beads.

6. Rituals provided in four variations: a) Meditation, b) Individual ritual, c) Two-person ritual, and d) Group ritual.

Before Beginning Your Practice

This book is both a manual and a ritual book. If you don't want to read it from cover to cover, use it freely, following your own interests. The second chapter provides instructions that can be useful for any kind of prayer beads. After reading it, follow your own interest in the choice of the tradition you want to practice. Keep in mind also that it is a good idea to experiment with traditions with which you are not familiar. Practice is a wonderful key that goes further than any theoretical or historical teaching. A ritual will teach you more in a short time than any intellectual study. It is not necessary for you to learn a tradition or a system before performing meditations and rituals. Just use the keys provided in this book and you will be surprised by the power and efficiency of the results.

The Four Traditions: Qabala, Hermeticism, Wicca, and Druidism

The ritual texts provided in this part allow you to have various spiritual experiences. Each one will help you go beyond the usual theoretical explanations. You will feel the essence of these Western traditions. You will be surprised by the understanding you will acquire, even without previous knowledge of these fields.

Furthermore, through regular use of these practices, you will be able to train your inner abilities and grow spiritually. This is one of the main goals.

The Pronunciations

The rituals contain several sacred words and mantras in various languages. Don't worry! I always provide a simple code for the pronunciations of these words. You can find in the appendix two charts (Hebrew and Greek) that give you the keys for the pronunciations. Then the reading of the phonetics used for Greek and Hebrew will be rapidly obvious to you.

Chapter 1

What Are Prayer Beads?

Prayer beads are powerful magical tools. Every magician, theurgist, or believer would benefit by using them regularly. A countless number of different prayer beads exist, but all are made of two things: a string and beads. Many other elements can be added, such as charms, shells, and other symbols. However, without a specific number of beads and a specific function, such a tool would simply be a jewel, beautiful but useless.

Prayer beads are used to count a number of prayers, sacred words, sounds, or mantras. Consequently, their structure is precise and always in relation to a spiritual symbolism. Their efficiency comes from the union of theology, ritual practices, and material support.

It is difficult to know exactly when necklaces began to be used differently from simple jewels. Necklaces or bracelets with beads were made at every step of human history, but not always used for ritual purposes. To know if such objects were used for a ritual or religious purpose requires proof. We can find clues when there is a specific pattern in the number or sequence of beads. Ancient representations showing someone carrying prayer beads in his hands can be a good indication of a special use. In order to identify such an artifact as prayer beads, we need a clear connection between its design and a spiritual belief or theology. A symbolic sequence of the number of beads can also be a good indication.

As mentioned in the Introduction, the goal of this book is not to write a history of prayer beads. This is why a few references will be enough to give you a comprehensible panorama of their existence.

An undeniable use of prayer beads can be found around the eighth century BCE in Hinduism (India). This religion uses prayer beads composed of 27, 56, or 108 beads. This is one of the religious tools that monks are allowed to possess. When Romans went to India, they witnessed the Hindus' followers declaiming their mantras with what was called "Japa Mala" in their hands. We don't know for sure if Pagans from the Mediterranean world ritually utilized what they called at this time a "Rosary," but undeniably, this ritual tool remains known by some closed groups.

Between the third and fifth centuries, the first Christians who lived in the desert of Egypt began to use knotted ropes to count their prayers. It is easy to see their logic in wanting to separate a religious tool from something that could be considered by these monks as a jewel, a wealthy possession. This tradition of the knotted ropes (of 33, 50, or 100 knots) remains today in the Eastern Orthodox Church.

As you may know, the Catholic Church uses what is called the "Rosary." It is the best-known set of prayer beads used since its first revelation by Saint Dominic, a famous Christian figure who lived in Italy during the thirteenth century. From then on, the Rosary was promoted by monks, priests, theologians, and popes. The prayers used with this Catholic set of prayer beads are always the "Our Father" and the "Hail Mary." Meditations were progressively associated with ritual pronunciations of the two main Catholic prayers. For seven centuries, this set of prayer beads spread into every group of people in the Catholic world.

When I was a child in France, Rosaries were everywhere in Catholic families like mine. This symbol was as present as the symbol of the cross. Rosaries were hung on walls, given as gifts at first communion or to the bride at a wedding, even placed between the hands of the dead before closing the coffin. Traditions like the latter are ageless, similar to ancient Egyptians placing amulets on the mummy before closing the sarcophagus.

In Europe, the Rosaries are usually bought at a place of pilgrimage and blessed by a priest. This way has always been spontaneous and unconscious. It is a real manifestation of a deep, atavistic, and magick behavior. When I was a child, I didn't ask about these things. I would just witness the behaviors of followers who took devoted care of these prayer beads.

These sacred emblems were used by Catholics during specific events and celebrations such as "Holy Friday" (two days before Easter), Sunday afternoon celebrations, etc. However, most of the time they were just the visual presence of a magick protection.

We will talk in another part of this book about the principles involved in the use of prayer beads. It is essential to understand them in order to use this tool with the best impact possible.

But some uses of the Rosary were more ritualistic. One of my grandmothers was Italian. For her, the Rosary was not just a magical tool placed in the house for protection. It was, above all, a devotional instrument.

Several times per day, she practiced a specific ritual. I was very young but I remember clearly the smell of the candles. She always half-closed the blinds to obtain a suitable darkness. She opened a silver triptych depicting the episodes of the passion of Christ. Then she lit a candle. Dipping her right fingers in a cup of blessed water, she performed the sign of the cross as Catholics do, took the Rosary, and began these long cycles of prayer.[3] Two times a day, she recited the short version with one prayer per bead for a total of fifty-nine prayers. One time per day, during the evening, she did the complete version, really called the "Rosary." The Rosary is composed of performing three times the basic prayer cycle of fifty-nine, for a total of 177 prayers. Each set was associated with a specific meditation and visualization. The full Catholic system is provided on my website[4] under the section "Prayer Beads."

At the heart of this ritual was the movement of the Rosary beads in my grandmother's hands and the repetitive whispering of the prayers. Of course, I was standing in her room in a country house in the southwest of France, but I could have been in a hovel in the center of Tibet, listening to the family

---

3. A Rosary has fifty-nine beads. Fifty-three beads are used to pronounce the prayer to Mary and six beads correspond to the prayer to the Father. More precisely, on the circle, there are five sets of ten "Hail Mary" beads separated by four single "Our Father" beads. On the pendant, there is one "Our Father" bead at each end of a set of three "Hail Mary" beads.

4. www.debiasi.org

prayers. It would have been exactly the same thing, the same kind of devotional ritual.

I remember the full Catholic assembly kneeling and murmuring the prayers of the Rosary. It was like being in a Tibetan monastery and listening to the mantras of a Buddhist assembly.

In America today, the presence of prayer beads is still very strong. This is true in South America, in Mexico, and in the Southern United States. The cars belonging to Catholics can be recognized by the large number of Rosaries hanging on the rearview mirrors. What to say when a large company such as Walmart sells Rosaries…

Even if this specific set of prayer beads is world-famous, it is important to keep in mind that it is not the only one that exists. As you will see later in this book, other prayer beads have been created in the past and associated with various devotions. This is the case, for example, with the Saint Michael prayer beads devoted to the archangels.

Prayer beads are universal in their use and purpose. No matter your religion, your belief, or your family tradition, prayer beads belong to a widespread ritual practice everyone can use. It is wonderful to learn how to experiment with this very useful tool and see how easy it is to be focused when you begin your practice.

What Is the Function of Prayer Beads in Religion and Magick?

As previously stated, it is easy to deduce how prayer beads can function in a religious perspective. But let's take a moment to consider this from an anthropologist's point of view. First of all, the function of religion is to connect us as humans with the divine. In order to obtain this result, religions usually use an intermediary called a priest (or priestess). In the Christian church, as in most religions, someone receives an initiation, a consecration that gives him a power superior over the people. This power allows him or her to celebrate rituals and create, by his expertise, a bridge between the divine plan and the people.

I am not saying here that such an intermediary, the priest, is indispensable if we want to raise our soul. Several other ways exist to be connected with the divine without such a mediator. I think, for example, of personal initiations, psychic training, inner development, meditations, prayers, magical tools, etc. Several initiatic Orders like the Ordo Aurum Solis teach processes that allow you to act by yourself.

Spirituality has always been regarded with mistrust by religious organizations. When you are eager to undertake a spiritual work, even in a religion, you are, in fact, building a personal and direct relation to the divine. Religious establishments are always trying to authorize this, to strongly frame this inner will. Prayer beads are at the heart of this invisible conflict. As a remarkable manifestation of the spiritual world, they are used and controlled by churches.

A clear indicator of this special character of the prayer beads is the way they appear. I explained before that these religious items have existed for a very long time. But they are not the result of a deliberate and well-planned strategy from the churches. They are revelations!

According to legend, the Catholic Rosary was revealed by an apparition of the Virgin Mary to Saint Dominic. Another monk, Dominic of Prussia, received the revelation of the meditations that are associated with the structure of this set of prayer beads.

In Portugal during the eighteenth century, the Archangel Saint Michael appeared to a nun, revealing another form of prayer beads. Examples like this are numerous and they show a direct action from the divine plan (or the unconscious of the devout) unveiling a specific religious tool or spiritual method. The consequence is always a rapid spread of this practice, quickly adopted by a large number of believers.

In a second step, the religious power intervenes to define the limits of the individual initiative. If we consider this process carefully, we can clearly recognize the authenticity of such religious revelations. The religion has no importance here, because I am talking about the process itself.

As you may know, meditation is an easy process to explain but a difficult inner exercise to master. Prayer can be seen as a specific way that can lead you to a deep contact with invisible plans. The connection you are trying to create between two worlds cannot be the result of a single prayer.

When you were a child, you learned how to walk or to speak through repetition. When someone wants to memorize a text, the usual method is to repeat it. Mastering such apprenticeship is going even further. You have to fully assimilate the text in order to forget it. At the end, as a good actor, you become the text itself.

To take another example, you walk and you do not forget the process of walking. This is the same thing here. The repetition of prayers will allow you to go through the veil of the Holy Mysteries. With multiple declamations you will effortlessly cross a mystical threshold. As someone who comes back to the surface of a lake, you will suddenly inhale pure air as if for the first time.

This is the effect you can reach if you are using the prayer beads with a religious perspective. When specific visualizations are associated with these pronunciations, as my grandmother was using, you will be able to obtain an inner understanding of these mysteries.

It is easy to understand that numbers are not chosen by chance. Even if they are the result of a revelation, they can always reveal a symbolic meaning. Considering these esoteric aspects, you will be able to progressively evolve from religion to magick. You will create a distance between your inner technique and the dogmas linked to the instrument you are using. Magick or High Magic gives you the opportunity to keep the best of such traditions. Being able to take a simple ritual tool such as prayer beads and make them powerful magical instruments still amazes me. The Western tradition teaches that the most powerful keys are always obvious. You just need a different view to recognize them and a clear training to know how to use them. This is what this book is about.

Chapter 2

Main Principles
for a Successful Practice

Every magician, theurgist, or believer would benefit from having tools such as prayer beads and using them regularly. This is a powerful magical instrument. The decision of buying or making is not so important. The essential point is to understand that you can consider prayer beads in two main ways:

1. They can express your feelings regarding the divine, your spiritual beliefs. In this case, they are something you will create following what you feel is the best for you. You can sometimes find people who will make unique prayer beads personalized for you. This is the way many magicians and Pagans manage prayer beads. They consider that the creative and intuitive aspects in the making are something important. This is true, but it relates to a specific kind of use. In this case it is quite impossible to connect the practice with specific mysteries. It is possible to

meditate and reach a different level of consciousness. But there are limits to the prayer beads' use.

2. Prayer beads can be considered according to a traditional symbolism. In this case, their creation is not arbitrary. Everything that comprises them is significant: the number of beads, their sequence, matter, color, medals, etc. All of these aspects are directly given by the tradition itself or derived from symbolic rules. As you have already understood, this book explains this second category of prayer beads.

It is now easier to answer the previous question: Make it or buy it?

In the first scenario, it is better to do it yourself if you are not totally sure of the psychic ability of the one who could do it for you.

In the second case, if you are not sure you have all the knowledge to build it according to the traditional teachings, buy it. Every detail of its making is important. I pay great attention to the matter of the beads. Let's take an example. Hermeticism and theurgy are related to the God Djehuti (Thoth). According to the ancient texts of this tradition, Djehuti wrote sacred words on tablets made of turquoise. Consequently, this stone became associated with this divinity and this tradition. If your goal is to work in connection with the egregore of this tradition, it will be better to use real turquoise. Of course you will be able to visualize Djehuti even using prayer beads made of obsidian. However, I can assure you that the link with his power will be more difficult to create and maintain.

We can say the same about the number of beads related to specific periods of the year and levels of consciousness. The energies you will use are clearly linked to the words, of course, but also to the number of pronunciations. The number and groups of numbers are provided by the string of prayer beads itself. This is why, in order to be efficient, it is better to use prayer beads symbolically made and corresponding to a specific use.

In this book I will always give you the two possibilities: order it or make it. That means I will give you the full description of the prayer beads associated with each exercise. If you want to make them, you will be able to do so according to the correct esoteric rules.

Power of the Egregore

The egregore is a very important aspect of religion and magick. Surprisingly, it is not too often found in the occult literature. In order to understand how mysterious tools like prayer beads can link you to specific egregores, it is essential to know exactly what they are.

To begin, an egregore is an invisible power, which is the result of a group working ritually. This egregore may progressively become autonomous and independent from its source. If you consider that you are composed of two parts, the spiritual (invisible part) and material (visible part), you can understand groups in the same way.

Any group is composed of visible and invisible bodies. I am talking here about invisible bodies, such as our auras, but also about spiritual creatures that can be attracted by these ritual gatherings. What we have to understand is that there is always more in a group than the mere sum of its parts. A ritual group—such as House Lodge, Coven, Chapter, and so on—gives birth all throughout its existence and during each of its ritual practices to a kind of independent creature. The latter then progressively develops its own unique character, thereby becoming more and more effective. Keep in mind that, at this point, this process is unconscious. This phenomenon is the same for magical, religious, or even political groups.

This egregore can be seen as a real entity, larger than any individual participant. It has also been called a "thought form" by occultist and medium Helena Blavatsky. Over the years, these archetypes somehow could become autonomous. This may be helpful or not, depending on whether the character of the group, and therefore the egregore, is well-balanced.

It is important to remember that every spiritual group has an egregore, because each participant is using invisible energies in his rituals. When a group works for a few years, these invisible energies become increasingly powerful.

When you are using prayers, songs, ritual tools, etc., belonging to a specific religious or spiritual tradition, you will be in relation to its egregore. You can compare that to the use of an electric appliance. You don't know anything about the way the electricity works and is provided to your house. You don't know anything about the functioning of this appliance. You just bought it. Then you plug it in and switch it on. The refrigerator or whatever starts receiving the electricity and working as it is supposed to. In this case there is no surprise. This is exactly the same when you use a ritual tool such as prayer beads. You have several different prayer beads, just as you have different appliances. The difference will be in relation to their function—for example, razor, vacuum cleaner, cooking pot, etc. There are also different models and efficiencies for each function—for example, several brands of razors, etc. This is the same for prayer beads. Some of them were created by Christians, other by Hermetists, Druids, and so on.

When you use prayer beads, you will be connected to a specific energy or egregore without noticing it. This process is good because you will benefit from the power that already exists. You want to do that. It will help you.

However, you don't want to be under the influence of invisible powers. Being aware of that, you will be able to use these ritual tools for your own well-being. The rituals provided in this book were prepared to give you the help of specific egregores but without being influenced by them. This is the best way to work.

Mantras, Prayers, and Sacred Sounds

Sounds can be seen as the heart of the prayer beads. Every spiritual tradition using this ritual tool associates it with precise pronunciations. Catholics use their two main prayers when they perform the ritual of the Rosary. It is the same in several Western spiritualities. However, when we use the word "mantras," we are thinking about the Eastern religions, such as Hinduism or Buddhism. This is true, but if we consider what a mantra is, we can go further and see how it applies to Western history. This concept can be used in the same way for the East and the West.

Mantras are sacred words, sounds, phonemes, hymns, and prayers used in a spiritual context to modify the state of consciousness, reaching a communion with an inward or outward divine. These pronunciations create a vibration that resonates in your flesh and at the same time activates your body of light, your inner energy. Pronouncing these "sacred sounds" is like playing a musical instrument. Something happens and affects the space where you are. The effects are not limited to you, but can have a visible and invisible impact. Then this vibration will liberate your soul and lead it to a higher level, in connection with the deities in relation to the sounds used.

In some cases, it is necessary to use repetitive sounds. I like to compare the result to drops of water dripping on a very strong stone. After years, the stone will be pierced. Repetition is essential and so it is for the spiritual practice of prayer beads. The rituals provided in this book often use the rhythmic pronunciation of sacred words or sounds. These sounds are considered sacred because they are used for a spiritual purpose. They can be seen as living symbols of the divine. As a symbol, each sound is the visible expression of the divine.

Thousands of years of experimentation have helped the initiates find these sounds. Because of religious war, this Egypto-Hellenistic heritage was destroyed and recycled centuries later in the Christian practices used by the desert monks. But truth never disappears totally and we are lucky today to still have in the West two essential elements: manuscripts and Theurgic orders. With this help it is possible to understand that the Western tradition is as efficient and alive as the Eastern tradition.

Two levels must be thought about when you consider the use of "Sacred Sounds": 1. your mind; 2. your breath.

Your Mind

The use of prayer beads can be considered as a meditation and a magical action. Depending on which ritual you choose, one or the other will be emphasized.

As you may know, meditation is difficult. It is not always easy to keep our mind calm, relaxed, and to avoid the agitation of our ideas. I would advise you to sit, breathe, relax, and calm your mind. This is the process you must follow. You might find that you can do it for a few seconds, a few minutes, and then the ideas come back and you lose your emptiness.

The Western tradition has developed another way to approach this goal. If I cannot empty my mind, let's fill it. If you move too fast and I want to slow you or even stop you, I ask you to go in the opposite direction. I am sure that you will stop running just to consider the information I gave you. This is the same process here. Your senses must not be totally abandoned. They are parts of the ritual practice.

Getting three senses involved is enough to achieve this goal. Then your mind will surrender. Prayer beads are perfect for that. You will take the string of beads in your hands and move ritually from one bead to another: touch. You will pronounce sacred words: hearing. You will visualize a single image or symbol: vision. You can even use candles and incense: smell.

To clear your mind, you have to keep these senses in your awareness. The point here is to not go from one to another. You must try to welcome the senses you are using without any distance. You must not say mentally: "I am feeling the beads." You just have to feel the beads. You must not say: "I can hear my voice." You just have to hear your voice. You are not at a distance from yourself. You are not seeing yourself from elsewhere. You are doing this ritual and you are all senses, nothing more. Then your mind will progressively clear without effort.

Meditation is always the first step you want to achieve. In a few minutes, you can experiment with it and feel it. You will have to continue the practice for a few months to be able to keep it up for a longer period.

After meditation, the second step consists of connecting your inner self to the divine levels you are invoking with your ritual. Remember that you are made of flesh and spirit. You have two bodies: one visible, one invisible. In order to be efficient, your practice must involve both levels.

I just discussed the physical plane. Working on the invisible level is the result of sound and visualization. The latter is an essential key for any magical practice. When a believer is using this tool, he doesn't need any training to master this ability. His faith gives him the content. He knows instinctively how to focus on the deity he worships. In the case of a magician or Theurgist, he learns a technique in order to control the phenomenon, the experience. Consequently, he must use the visualization and keep it under control. In order to do that you must follow the indication provided in the rituals.

When I use the word "visualization" at this phase of the work, don't reduce its meaning to the construction of a mental picture. It can be, but it is more of a way to focus on an idea, trying to keep it in your mind for a while. When you are thinking of a place you know, you are not creating a picture *per se*. You are just focusing your mind on it, activating this mental representation. The visual details can appear if you decide to go further than the selection of the idea.

As you will see, the first step of the meditation will help you master the second step I just explained. When the ritual gives you a specific visualization, use it and try to stay focused on it, avoiding any tension. If you have no indications regarding what to keep in mind during the practice, just use the meditation as described before.

Your Breath

The use of vowels, words, or hymns is based on your breath. Obviously, your breath will play an essential role in the pronunciations of "sacred sounds." Initiatic Orders give specific attention to the way you breathe, and so do I in this book.

In the Eastern tradition, the technique related to the breath is called "Pranayama." This word means "extension of the breath" or "extension of the energy of life." This process has a very deep impact on your body and brain.

When I was young, for several years I practiced daily the Pranayama techniques taught by Yogi Swatmarama. The result was amazing and radically changed my perception of the world. It cleansed my body and the channels of energy, called in India "nadis." My physical energy increased, along with the light of my aura and astral body.

When I was performing these daily practices, it was even possible to experiment with what can be called paranormal manifestations all around me. Several years later, I was very surprised to find similar techniques taught in the Western tradition. They were not as precise as in yoga and were often implicit in various rituals, such as the pronunciations of the sacred sounds.

In order for you to perform such practices, you can use the two following simple techniques:

1. I recommend linking your breathing to your ritual in a specific way. When you inhale, build your visualization. While holding the air in your lungs, you intensify the mental representation. Then when you exhale and hold your lungs empty, forget your visualization, feeling only the air flowing out. It is interesting and important to practice for some time like that and see how you feel. I have seen many students and initiates use this technique with a lot of benefits. Their ability to visualize generally increases quickly without much effort.[5]

2. "Wave breathing" is a technique that uses only inhaling and exhaling without any holding (full or empty lungs). When unique sounds such as vowels are used as mantra, inhalation is silent and the exhalation is accomplished while vibrating the sound. In this case, every time you exhale, you pronounce the sound.

The speed of these repetitions depends on the goal, but it is important to be careful in using this technique alone. I recommend you not do this exercise too fast.[6] Instead, choose a relaxed and regular rhythm. In the case of a simple word com-

---

5. This is one of the breathing techniques used in the Ordo Aurum Solis.
6. This kind of hyperventilation can cause a decrease in the amount of a gas in the blood and may make you feel light-headed, have a rapid heartbeat, and be short of breath.

posed of at least of two syllables, the first one is pronounced when you inhale, and the second when you exhale.

In the exercises provided in this book, I will indicate how to pronounce when this is necessary. You can also listen to the pronunciations online on my personal website on the pages linked to this book.

Finally, when your practice is more advanced, you will be able to add the full wave breathing technique. Three parts of your body have to be considered when you inhale and exhale: abdomen, belly, and chest. First, move your lower abdomen, beginning at the top of your pubic bone. After filling the abdomen, focus on your belly, stretch your diaphragm, and continue with the third section, your chest. Feel that this movement is like a wave coming from the lower part of your abdomen up to your collarbones.

Do the same when you exhale. It is better to go slowly and regularly.

The processes combining these breathing techniques and the pronunciation of sacred sounds, also called mantras, can be summarized thusly:

- Hymn or prayer: Establish the rhythmic breathing for a few minutes, associate the visualization of the deity if there is one, take your prayer beads, and begin the practice of breathing as naturally as possible.

- Name or sound: Proceed in the same way, but instead breathe naturally with the prayer beads; use the wave breathing as indicated in the ritual.

Rituals

Our lives are full of rituals. When you wake up, eat breakfast, take a shower, etc., you are following a set of little rituals that constitute your day. Your psyche needs these points of reference. They keep you balanced. Of course, this is sometimes too much and these rituals can become real barriers, capable of imprisoning you: You will lose the ability to welcome unexpected things. Your horizon will diminish. Being aware of these risks can help you keep the best and avoid the worst.

Spiritual rituals can be considered in the same way. You can perform a single ritual and it could be great. However, in order to help you, it needs to become a real part of yourself. The ritual tool, the prayer beads, must become personal. This is why you have to consecrate the beads. Then, as my grandmother was doing with the Rosary practice, you will have to plan a daily, or at least regular, individual ritual. I recommend choosing a ritual in this book and performing it during a precise and symbolic period. A moon cycle or a zodiac sign are very good. They will even help you in this process. If you choose the moon cycle, it is best to begin the first day of the new moon.[7] For a zodiac sign, begin the cycle the first day of the sign.

How to Keep Your Prayer Beads

If we put so much emphasis on a spiritual tool like this one, we have to consider it something special. The notion of "sacred" can be considered as something "put aside," "separated" from the common world. Prayer beads we are using in sacred rituals are progressively considered sacred tools. You are the

---

7. I wrote extensively about the cycle of the week and moon in my book *Rediscover the Magick of the Gods and Goddesses.*

only one who can decide what degree of sacredness you want to put in them.

When your prayer beads are not only for ornament but for practice, my advice is to use a pouch and to put the beads inside it between rituals. If you have different prayer beads related to various traditions, don't put them in contact with each other. Avoid putting them in someone else's hands. This is not a problem when you receive them, but after the blessing and even more so when you are using the beads, it is best to keep them for yourself. However, it is not a problem if someone sees the beads.

I have received several emails asking what to do if someone touches the beads without your consent. Understandably, a child can find the string of beads and manipulate it. There is a simple answer and this is true no matter what kind of magical tool we are talking about: You have to consider the person's motivation. If it is simple curiosity or a mistake, their handling of the beads is not a problem. It is best to pronounce a short blessing on the beads and this will be enough. If someone really uses the string of beads without your consent, then perform again the full ritual of blessing as described in this book.

If handling of the beads was done with a bad intention, such as to defy you, my advice is to throw the string of beads in a river or sea and buy a new one. If someone stole it, don't worry; be confident in the positive result of the energy you put inside. My experience shows me we have to be careful with bad energies and it is better not to underestimate a bad intention.

Solitary, Two-person, and Group Use of the Prayer Beads
It is a specialty of this book to present each ritual in four aspects: 1. simple meditation, 2. individual ritual, 3. couple ritual, and 4. group ritual. In fact, such uses of prayer beads are obvious. For anyone who sees someone praying alone or in a religious assembly, this question doesn't even exist. Clearly, you can pray alone or in a group. However, the intent of this book is to give you a Theurgic or magick process to go beyond religion.

The rituals provided in this book can help you go forward more efficiently than a simple religious habit. The point is not just to pray together. The goal is to perform a ritual that may help you to ascend to the divine plane in relation to the prayer beads you are using. This is what is called a "Theurgic ritual," and why you must train yourself through the various steps mentioned earlier.

It may be best not to begin the rituals immediately, but to carefully read the whole chapter and practice the meditation. Then focus on the individual ritual and practice it during at least one cycle (moon or astrological sign). When you have practiced it several times without hesitating during the process, you can go forward and begin to use it as a couple and in a group.

When I am talking about use as a couple (called in the book "two-person ritual"), I am not limiting my talk to straight couples composed of a man and a woman. In these rituals, a couple is just an assembly of two persons, regardless of gender or relationship status.

When you read the ritual for the first time, you may think it is a bit complex. In fact, even if the description is detailed, the structure of the ritual itself is logical and well-structured. After a first reading, I suggest that you, as an individual or couple, practice it without really doing it. It will be a good opportunity to put this text in motion. Then choose a good time, following any of the suggestions provided. Don't forget to reverse the roles, because most of the time one is acting and the second is more passive, receiving the energy.

Doing the ritual in a group is interesting and can contribute to a deeper ritualistic experience. You can consider a group to consist of at least three persons. A bigger number is even better, considering the amount of energy the group will generate. Here again, you can try to have an equal number of males and females. If this balance is impossible, forget it and proceed anyway.

I recommend a few practice runs before actually performing the ritual. When a group work is planned and performed there are two major tendencies: 1. keeping the same director every time; 2. performing the ritual once only.

It is good for the group occasionally to switch this function of director. When the same person is always in charge, a kind of imbalance occurs, which is bad for everyone. Switching this role allows the volunteers to experiment from a different point of view.

The second point is also very important. I talked previously about the power generated by a succession of daily practices. This routine creates a regular wave of energy on the invisible level. If the goal is to contact a specific spiritual plane in order to receive something from it, regular practices are paramount. This is as true for an individual as it is for a group.

Of course, working daily in a group is a real challenge in our modern life.

In past years I experimented with the weekly sequence of rituals in different contexts. This is very effective and I recommend this rhythm. If you want to experiment with this kind of cycle, I recommend using the cycle of the moon as a reference. You can choose the four phases of the moon. If this is not possible, pick a specific day during the waxing moon. Then continue with the next one seven days later, and so on. It is always interesting and efficient to associate cycles of rituals with the cycles of the moon.

Chapter 3

Consecration of Your
Prayer Beads

Blessings have been part of spiritual work for a very long time. In most of the largest religions, blessings are often performed by clerics. In the case of initiatic Orders and other magical approaches, anyone is considered able to perform rituals and consecrate items without being obligated to accept a precise dogma from a religious hierarchy. Of course, it is also possible to train yourself in order to perform such sacred mysteries. Anyone can learn to drive on his own. But it is clearly safer, faster, and more efficient to learn it in the friendly environment of an initiatic tradition.

Everyone has the ability to consecrate ritual items and you can begin your practice and training right now. In order to be as efficient as possible, this process of consecration is rooted on the number 8.[8]

---

8. This is the number of the sacred Ogdoad of the Mysteries related to the God Djehuti (Thoth), founder of the Hermetic and Theurgic traditions.

These principles are: 1. Cleaning; 2. Delimitation; 3. Dedication; 4. Attraction; 5. Blessing; 6. Naming; 7. Activation; 8. Sealing.

It is important to give you the essential meaning of each of these ritual steps.

1. *Cleaning:* The goal of this ritual step is to clean the aura of the item in order to recover the original state of the object. Suppose you ordered prayer beads. Someone shaped the beads and sent them to the company, which assembled them in the shape of the precise prayer beads you received. All along this process, people touched the item and handled it. They put inside it a part of their own auras, thoughts, and history. All this is not bad *per se*. This is just different from you. So the first goal is to wash away these invisible memories.

2. *Delimitation:* When the prayer beads are clean regarding vibrations, you have to isolate them from outer influences. In order to do that you will create "delimitation." Casting the magical circle is a good representation of this step.

3. *Dedication:* In order to be efficient, a ritual must begin with a dedication. When the space has been cleaned and separated from the outside, it is time to pronounce a specific formula. This is intended to explain the purpose of the ceremony in a few precise words. This ritual declamation will act as a key, opening the gate to the following steps. This declaration will also help your energy to be focused on the action you are trying to accomplish.

4. *Attraction:* After opening the door to the invisible plane, you will attract and invoke the divine powers. Many things are used during this step to obtain this result. Candles, talismans, medals, incenses, etc., are symbols and magical tools that are used for this purpose. Magick uses the law of sympathy of relationship between symbols and spiritual powers. For example, a gold jewel will attract the power of the spiritual sun, and specific incense will do the same in regard to a divinity. These powers can be attracted around us in order to be used in the following steps. They can be also attracted inwardly. In this case we will become a channel for these powers.

5. *Blessing:* The apex of the ceremony is the Blessing. You can also call this step the "consecration." The powers we just invoked are now focused on the object. Declamations are used for this purpose, along with the drawing of sacred signatures and symbols.

6. *Naming:* Ritual tools such as the prayer beads are dedicated to someone in particular. This is the same process if you do the ritual for yourself or for someone else. You must create a real link between this object and the individual for whom it is prepared. For that you have to ceremonially name the owner. This verbalization establishes a link between the prayer beads and its owner on the invisible plane.

7. *Activation:* The activation is an interesting phase we can find in the Ogdoadic and Theurgic rituals. Once the powers have been introduced in the prayer beads, you must start. In order to understand, let's take the example of a car. When the car is brand-new and clean, the first thing

you do if you want to use it is fill the tank. This is what you did in the previous steps. After that, you have to turn the key and start the engine. This is what you are doing in this step. This ritual activation is done by speaking directly to the sacred item. This may seem strange, but the belief is that the presence of the spiritual power inside it gives it a kind of life of potential consciousness you must awaken.

8. *Sealing:* The last step consists of sealing the whole process. As you pour liquid wax on a letter to close it, you have to do the same in your ritual. This ritual conclusion accomplishes two things: 1. seals the link created between you and the prayer beads; 2. maintains the spiritual powers you invoked inside the object.

Having followed this whole process, you will have in your hands a very powerful magical tool you will cherish with pride and humility.

Blessing of Your Prayer Beads

Perform this blessing if you want to immediately use your prayer beads. Even shorter than the consecration, this is an efficient process. You can use it no matter what specific prayer beads you want to consecrate.

Blessing of Water

I recommend choosing mineral water instead of water from your faucet.

Light a candle made of beeswax.

Pour half of the water you want to consecrate in a large cup.

Then hold the bottle (or carafe) and say:

Coming from Okeanos, the waters of the four directions flow toward us and meet together in this sacred space recreating the world of the origins from which we came.

Pour in four increments the other half of the water.
Replace the carafe and take the sea salt.
Drop a few grains of salt in the water, while saying:

This salt represents the true purifying essence of the primeval waters.

Take the candle and with it, draw a cross and a circle around the cross above the surface of water. Then plunge the flame of the candle into the center of the cup to extinguish the flame. At the same time, say:

May the flames that were united with the primeval waters be activated by this union.

Replace the candle.
Continue saying:

By the powers of the hidden breath, may this water reveal its power!

Then blow four times on the surface of the water at the center of the cup.
Extend your hands in the direction of the water, palms down, a few inches above the surface.
Conclude by saying:

> **May this original water that constitutes the**
> **thread of everything be fully consecrated**
> **and capable to purify everything.**
> **So mote it be!**

Then you can use this water and store it protected from the light. Do not drink it. This consecrated water is intended to be used only in rituals or for any purification you need.

Blessing Prayer

Here is the blessing prayer you can use for all the prayer beads described in the book. This prayer is provided with the explanations of the gestures you can use.

The prayer beads are placed on a white fabric in front of you.

Sprinkle the prayer beads with the consecrated water. While doing this, say:

> **May this original water that constitutes**
> **the thread of everything purify these**
> **prayer beads.**

Put the prayer beads in the palm of your hands and lower your hands to the height of your thighs (this will be the height for Earth in the ritual). Then begin the following invocation. At each step you will raise your hands. Water will be the height of your belly; the Air, your chest; the Fire, the height of your forehead; and the Aether, maximum height you can reach in front of you.

I invoke the powers of Earth, Water, Air, and Fire!
I invoke the power of Aether!

Lower your hands to the height of your heart and say:

May these prayer beads be consecrated
by the power of the golden sun.

Visualize a pure golden light descending from the sky to the top of your head and going to the center of your chest. Visualize yourself surrounded by a sphere of golden light.

Then say:

I am the Sun!
I am the wheel moved by the Fire!
I am the center of the power which moves the spheres!

Close your hands with the prayer beads inside. Breathe deeply while you increase the light all around you and, more precisely, in the prayer beads you hold between your palms.

Take at least five cycles of breath, then say:

May these prayer beads be immersed
in the pure golden rays of the sun!
May these prayer beads become a living
spiritual creature!
May these prayer beads become the key opening
the egregore of the tradition he belongs to!
May these prayer beads become the instrument

that links me to the divine!
May these prayer beads become the manifestation
of the Divine Beings I wish to pray to!

Breathe in silence for few minutes and bring the prayer beads into the palm of your left hand.

May the divine Order of the cosmos
harmonize all aspects of your life!
May the powers of the stars lead your life
to a successful realization!
May the skies be propitious to you in
all aspects of your life!
By the power of the elements and the divine,
I bless you!
So mote it be!

With your right index finger, draw a pentagram of invocation[9] upon the prayer beads.

The consecration is done and you can now store the prayer beads in their bag.

Consecration of Beads

You can use this consecration with many benefits. It is not necessary to use both this one and the previous short process. Although, if you wish to do so, you can begin with the previous consecration and then proceed to this one.

---

9. Illustrations and other diagrams can be found on my website (www. debiasi.org) and in the app about the book.

Materials

The prayer beads

Anointing oil (specifically chosen according the tradition of the prayer beads, or olive oil)

Incense Purification (specific or myrrh)

Eight candles (white or beeswax)

Consecrated water in a bowl

Sea salt

A printing with the symbol of a double square

White altar cloth

The best way to proceed to this benediction is to choose the day of the full moon and to face its direction. If you cannot see the moon, just face East.

Install everything according to the description presented here.

Step 1: Cleaning

Light the candles clockwise. You begin with the first candle at the top of the figure, closest to the moon (or the East).

In order to invoke the divine powers and to welcome them into your inner being, into your aura, stand up in front of your altar and visualize above your head the symbol of an eight-pointed star. Hold this glorious symbol in your mind, raise your arms up to the sky, palms up, and declaim one time:

En Giro Torte Sol Ciclos Et Rotor Igne
(ain giro tortai sol tchiklos ait rotor ignai) [10]

Lower your arms, allowing them to hang naturally at your sides.
Spread a few grains of salt on the prayer beads, saying:

**May this salt purify these beads and bring
back their original balance and power.**

Spread a few drops of consecrated water on the prayer beads,
saying:

**May this sacred water purify these beads and bring
back their original balance and power.**

Light the incense. Hold the beads eight times in the smoke of
the incense, saying:

**May this incense purify these beads and bring back
their original balance and power.**

Replace the censer to its initial position.
Bring the prayer beads to the vertical of each candle in the
same sequence you did when you lighted the candles, saying:

---

10. This mantra can be translated as followed: "I am the sun, I am this wheel
    moved by fire, its twist causes the spheres to rotate." Even if this mantra
    is a mix of Latin and old Italian, the pronunciations provided can be
    found in the Hebrew chart provided in the Appendix. It is also called
    "Ogdoadic Invocation."

**May this fire purify these beads and bring
back their original balance and power.**

Replace the prayer beads to the center of the symbol.

Step 2: Delimitation

Take the censer. Add another incense cone (or incense) if this is
needed. Then make eight circles clockwise around the candles.

While you are doing that, visualize a transparent wall of
light all around the beads.

Then replace the censer.

Step 3: Dedication

Close your eyes and open your arms in the direction of the
sky. Then say:

**On this day, I ... *say your name* ... perform this ritual
of consecration of these prayer beads in order to connect my inner self to the divine plane.**

**I solemnly swear to keep the beads separated from all
mundane life and to use the beads as a sacred tool for
the devotion of the divine.**

**May these true words be heard in all worlds and
recognize my dedication to his Great Work.**

Take the prayer beads in your hands, put them in contact with
the center of your chest, kneel in silence, and feel the creation
of a strong link between the beads and you.

After few minutes of silence, stand up, keeping the prayer beads in your hands.

Step 4: Attraction

Place your hands in front of you with the prayer beads maintained as an offering on the top of the palms, turned to the sky, and declaim:

**I invoke the powers of the seven skies
upon these prayer beads.**

Then sing the seven sacred vowels in ascending tones:

1. A (the Greek letter Alpha—Pronounced as "a" in *father*—D)
2. E (the Greek letter Epsilon—Pronounced as "e" in *set*—E flat)
3. H (the Greek letter Eta—Pronounced as "a" in *care*—F)
4. I (Greek letter Iota—Pronounced as "e" in *meet*—G)
5. O (Greek letter Omicron—Pronounced as "o" in *hot*—A flat)
6. U (Greek letter Upsilon—Pronounced as "u" in *Crème Brûlée*—B)
7. O (Greek letter Omega—Pronounced as "o" in *only*—C)

Step 5: Blessing

Visualize a powerful golden light going from your hands to the prayer beads and from the sky to the beads. Raise your hands slightly in the direction of the sky while you increase the light. Keep this position and pronounce eight times the invocation:

En Giro Torte Sol Ciclos Et Rotor Igne

Lower your arms. Replace the prayer beads in the center of the candles. Take the oil and with your right finger, anoint each bead in silence.

Replace the oil. Extend your arms in the direction of the prayer beads, palms facing them, visualizing a powerful light all around them.

Step 6: Naming
Bring the prayer beads into the palm of your left hand. Put your right palm upon them and say:

> **I ... *say your name* ... solemnly declare that these prayer beads are consecrated today for the spiritual use of ... *say the name of the person for whom you are performing this ritual (or replace that with "for my spiritual use")* ...**

> **May these prayer beads be linked with ......**
> ***proceed with the name as you just did* ...**
> **So mote it be!**

Replace the prayer beads on your altar in the center of the candles.

Step 7: Activation

Cross your arms, right on left, bend down your head, and say:

> **Hear now, O my prayer beads!**
> **You have been cleaned, purified, and consecrated.**
> **You have been presented to the highest divine**
> **powers and irradiated by the sacred light of the sun.**
> **I recognize in you the power to help me**
> **in my spiritual quest!**

(Optional:You can now decide to use the prayer beads for the first time in a cycle you will choose in the next chapters of the book.)

Step 8: Sealing

Stay silent and receptive for a while.

Draw a circled cross above the prayer beads, extend your arms, palms down, in the beads' direction and say:

> **I proclaim these prayer beads a bond with the divine**
> **world and protector of the one to whom they are des-**
> **tined!**
> **So mote it be!**

Extinguish the candles in the reverse sequence of the lighting and say:

> **May this spiritual light continue to**
> **enlighten my body of light!**

You can now store the prayer beads in their bag.

Chapter 4

Qabalistic Tradition

Qabalah is an explanation of the universe that is deeply rooted in the Jewish tradition and the Bible. However, throughout the centuries various groups and individuals have made use of this spiritual system apart from its original tradition. These developments adapted and used the Qabalah in many specific ways. Today we have Christian Qabalah, Magick Qabalah, Hermetic Qabalah, etc. After several centuries of use, these different interpretations are as valid as the original Hebrew system.

The use of prayer beads rooted in this tradition gives you the opportunity to immediately undertake a practical exploration of this system. This was the case in the first Rose-Cross group to exist in modern times (Kabbalistic Order of the Rose-Cross). The use of the sacred names and letters, associated with specific visualizations, allows you to deeply connect to this heritage, in the fullness of its power. Remember that you do not have to learn the Hebrew alphabet or the entirety of the system to use these prayer beads and rituals. It is all accessible now and you will be surprised to learn that you can quickly understand the structure of Qabalah from these rituals rather than from years of reading and study. As expected, each ritual has its own purpose, which you can use for your immediate benefit.

Ritual of the Blazing Wheel

This first ritual is part of the tradition of the Christian Qabalah. It was developed within the Kabbalistic Order of the Rose-Cross (KORC) as an interpretation of the famous engraving by Reuchlin, *The Rose Cross*. The founder of the KORC, Stanislas de Guaita, commented several times on this famous image, leading to the creation of this ritual. It is still part of the KORC's practices and is also used in Europe by Martinist Orders that practice magic.

I first observed this rite in the 1980s in an initiatic Order that was an heir to the Templar and Martinist[11] traditions. It took me a few years, but I was eventually able to obtain the complete details of this ritual, the concepts behind it, and the techniques that make it so powerful. It is those details I'll be sharing with you.

Purpose

Among the various benefits of this ritual are: development of the intuition, harmonization of your occult being to the cosmos (microcosm vs. macrocosm), contact with the archetypes of the Qabalistic and Magical traditions, harmonization with the egregore of the Kabbalistic Order of the Rose-Cross, and activation of the various levels of your aura.

---

11. Tradition founded by the French mystic Louis-Claude de Saint-Martin. This tradition was revived by the Kabbalistic Order of the Rose-Cross and then by the famous French occultist Papus.

Description of the Prayer Beads

The prayer beads for this ritual are identical to the Catholic Rosary with few essential differences. The Catholic Rosary is composed of fifty-nine beads, separated in five groups of ten beads and, between each series, one separating bead. A final string with four beads is separate from the circle. In Catholicism, different religious representations are included in the design. Generally this is the representation of Jesus on the Cross and his mother, Mary.

In the Rose-Cross tradition of the KORC, these two Catholic representations are absent. Instead, three ribbons of white, red, and black are connected to a pin or medal depicting the main symbol of the Kabbalistic Order of the Rose-Cross. The number of beads stays the same, even though their colors are codified to correspond to the alchemical correspondences.

Symbolism, Numbers, and General Process

The pentagram shows the relation between the four Hebrew letters and the four elements. The fifth is the Aether, the spirit. These series can be summarized in the following charts.

Symbolism Used During the First Cycle
of the Individual Ritual—World of Briah

In the following series, the first indication is the name of the letter, the second the element, and the third the color in Briah[12] to visualize.

1st series of 10 beads: Yod— △ Fire—red

2nd series of 10 beads: He— ▽ Water—blue

---

12. Briah is one of the four worlds defined by the Hebrew Qabalah.

3rd series of 10 beads: Shin— ✸ Aether—bright white light

4th series of 10 beads: Vav— △ Air—yellow

5th series of 10 beads: He— ▽ Earth—dark brown

Series of ten beads: Each letter is vibrated ten times while visualizing the specific color all around you.

Separating beads: The sacred name of Yeshua is vibrated while visualizing a bright light all around you.

Symbolism Used During the Second Cycle of the Individual Ritual

In the following series, the first indication is the name of the sephirah, and the second the symbol in Briah to visualize.

6th series: Malkuth—Young woman wearing a crown and seated on a throne

7th series: Yesod—Ithyphallic young man

8th series: Hod—Hermaphrodite

9th series: Netzach—Naked horsewoman

10th series: Tiphareth—Solar king

11th series: Geburah—Armed warrior-king on his chariot

12th series: Chesed—Priest-king on his throne

13th series: Binah—Celestial queen

14th series: Chokmah—Bearded patriarch

15th series: Kether—Old bearded king seen in profile

Series of ten beads: The name of each sephirah is vibrated ten times while visualizing the specific figures in front of you.

Separating beads: The twenty-two letters of the Hebrew alphabet will be vibrated on each separating bead while visualizing a circle of light around you.

Meditation

(The tools for the meditation are optional. However, it is always better, if you can, to use at least a candle.)

Hang a representation of the engraving by H. Khunrath in front of you. In front of it, place a white or plain beeswax candle and the required prayer beads for this ritual.

Sit comfortably facing East, take your prayer beads, and breathe peacefully for a few minutes.

Use successively the four separating beads that are on the string outside the circle.

On the first bead, say:

In front of me, in the East, I invoke you, Raphael (Rafaail)!

On the second bead, say:

Behind me, in the West, I invoke you, Gabriel!

On the third bead, say:

At my right, in the South, I invoke you, Haniel!

On the fourth bead, say:

At my left, in the North, I invoke you, Michael (Mikhaail)!

Use now the other beads that are in the circle. On the separating beads pronounce the name "**Yeshua**" once. On the series of beads, pronounce successively the Hebrew letters of his name, Yod, He, Shin, Vav, He.

Here is the detailed sequence:

First separating bead: **Yeshua (iaichooha)**

First series of ten beads: **Yod (iod)** (ten times, one per bead)

Second separating bead: **Yeshua**

Second series of ten beads: **He (hai)** (ten times, one per bead)

Third separating bead: **Yeshua**

Third series of ten beads: **Vav** (ten times, one per bead)

Fourth separating bead: **Yeshua**

Fourth series of ten beads: **Shin (chin)** (ten times, one per bead)

Fifth separating bead: **Yeshua**

Fifth series of ten beads: **He (hai)** (ten times, one per bead)

At the end of the five series, take the medal (or the ribbons) in your hand and pronounce the letters of the divine name in four series:

First: Yod—He—Vav—He

Second: Yod—He—Vav

Third: Yod—He

Fourth: Yod

Stay silent and receptive for a while, then stand up, put the prayer beads aside, and extinguish the candle, saying:

May this light continue to shine in the depths of my being!

Individual Ritual
Tools

Hang a representation of the engraving by H. Khunrath [13] in front of you. In front of it, place a white or plain beeswax candle and the required prayer beads for this ritual.

Opening

Light the candle. Take the prayer beads in your left hand and touch the pin or the medal with the forefinger of your right hand. Close your eyes and relax for a few minutes. You can stand up, sit on a chair, or take your usual meditation position.

Be aware of your body, your feet, and their contact with the ground. Keep your breathing slow and deep while you gradually relax. Concentrate on what you hear, what you feel, etc. As you become more aware of your own being, any disturbing

---

13. Heinrich Khunrath (1560–1605) was a German physician, hermetic philosopher, alchemist, and Qabalist. See my website (www.debiasi.org) for more details and for an image of the engraving.

thoughts or distractions will progressively disappear without having to worry about them.

Now imagine that you are in the center of a double circle. The place is quiet and peaceful, and the air around you is clear and crisp. Mentally looking around you, notice that the double circle is actually the center of a double sphere in which you stand. Looking up, you see that this double sphere is filled with the seven colors of the rainbow, which peacefully shimmer and sparkle around you. Whether you are actually standing or not, visualize that you are standing at the center of this space.

Then vibrate the following mystical names:

Cholem Yesodoth (kholeum iaisodot)

Ashim (achim)

Sandalphon (sandalfon)

Adonai Malekh (adonaï meleukh)

Stay silent for a few moments, feeling the presence of the divine powers of the sphere of Malkuth in which you stand.

The Establishment of the Guardians
The four beads

On the string of four beads do the following:

First bead: Move the thumb and index finger of your right hand on the first bead. Be aware of a yellow-colored light in front of you. Within this color, visualize Raphael with two pristine white wings, wearing a long green-gray robe. In one hand he carries a little box made of wood, ivory, and precious metal. His other hand holds the hand of a young child carrying a big fish.

While you increase this visualization, vibrate the sacred name **Raphael (Rafaail)**.

Second bead: Move the thumb and index finger of your right hand on the second bead. Be aware of lavender light behind you. Within this color, visualize Gabriel with two pristine white wings, wearing a bluish-white robe. He holds a ruby-red lamp.

While you increase this visualization, vibrate the sacred name **Gabriel (Gabriail)**.

Third bead: Move the thumb and index finger of your right hand on the third bead. Be aware of a clear turquoise light on your right. Within this color, visualize Haniel with two pristine white wings, wearing a long pink robe. He carries white roses in his arms.

While you increase this visualization, vibrate the sacred name **Haniel (Haniail)**.

Fourth bead: Move the thumb and index finger of your right hand on the fourth bead. Be aware of a clear, apricot-colored light on your left. Within this color, visualize Michael with two pristine white wings, wearing a long white-golden dress. He holds a palm in one hand and a white flag with a red cross in the other. A dragon is near him.

While you increase this visualization, vibrate the sacred name **Michael (Mik*h*aail)**.

First Cycle: Yeshua

The first decade: Put your thumb and forefinger on the first separating bead (right at the top of the string you just used). Breathe slowly, and mentally build an image of the Hebrew letters of the name in front of you: **Yeshua (iaichooha)**. If you do not wish to visualize the letters, just think of this sacred name. Then vibrate or pronounce the name Yeshua once.

Then take the first bead of the first series as you did for the previous beads. Visualize before you the Hebrew letter Yod[14] in red. After a few moments of silence, vibrate the name Yod.

While keeping the letter and color in your mind, take the second bead of this series and vibrate for a second time the Hebrew letter Yod.

Continue in the same way for the ten beads of this series.

The second decade: Proceed as you did for the first decade.

Separating bead: **Yeshua (iaichooha)**.

Ten beads of the series: Hebrew letter **He (hai)**, blue.

The third decade: Proceed as before.

Separating bead: Yeshua.

Ten beads of the series: Hebrew letter **Shin (chin)**, bright white.

The fourth decade: Proceed as before.

Separating bead: Yeshua.

Ten beads of the series: Hebrew letter **Vav**, yellow.

The fifth decade: Proceed as before.

Separating bead: Yeshua.

Ten beads of the series: Hebrew letter **He (hai)**, dark brown.

---

14. The representations of the Hebrew letters can be found in the Appendix.

Second Cycle: The Qabalistic Tree

The sixth decade: Put your thumb and forefinger on the next separating bead. Breathe slowly and clear your mind of any specific visualization. Then successively pronounce all the letters of the Hebrew alphabet: Alef, Bet, Gimel, Dalet, He, Vav, Zayin, Het, Tet, Yod, Kaf, Lamed, Mem, Nun, Samekh, Ayin, Pe, Tsadi, Qof, Resh, Shin, Tav.

Then take the first bead of the series again. Visualize before you the magical image of the sphere as provided in the second chart of symbolism of this cycle: A young woman wearing a crown and seated on a throne.

After a few moments of silence, vibrate the name of this sphere: **Malkuth (mal*kh*oot).**

While keeping this image in your mind, take the second bead of this series and vibrate for a second time the Hebrew word **Malkuth.**

Continue in the same way for the ten beads of this series.

The seventh decade: Proceed as before.

Separating bead: The twenty-two letters of the Hebrew alphabet.

Ten beads of the series: Visualization: Ithyphallic young man. Name of the Sphere: **Yesod (iaisod).**

The eighth decade: Proceed as before.

Separating bead: The twenty-two letters of the Hebrew alphabet.

Ten beads of the series: Visualization: Hermaphrodite. Name of the Sphere: **Hod (od).**

The ninth decade: Proceed as before.

Separating bead: The twenty-two letters of the Hebrew alphabet.

Ten beads of the series: Visualization: Naked horse-woman. Name of the Sphere: **Netzach (naitzach)**.

The tenth decade: Proceed as before.

Separating bead: The twenty-two letters of the Hebrew alphabet.

Ten beads of the series: Visualization: Solar king. Name of the Sphere: **Tiphareth (tifairait)**.

The eleventh decade: Proceed as before.

Separating bead: The twenty-two letters of the Hebrew alphabet.

Ten beads of the series: Visualization: Armed warrior-king on his chariot. Name of the Sphere: **Geburah (gaivoora)**.

The twelfth decade: Proceed as before.

Separating bead: The twenty-two letters of the Hebrew alphabet.

Ten beads of the series: Visualization: Priest-king on his throne. Name of the Sphere: **Chesed (khaisaid)**.

The thirteenth decade: Proceed as before.

Separating bead: The twenty-two letters of the Hebrew alphabet.

Ten beads of the series: Visualization: Celestial queen. Name of the Sphere: **Binah (bina)**.

The fourteenth decade: Proceed as before.

Separating bead: The twenty-two letters of the Hebrew alphabet.

Ten beads of the series: Visualization: Bearded patriarch. Name of the Sphere: **Chokmah (kho*kh*ma)**.

The fifteenth decade: Proceed as before.

Separating bead: The twenty-two letters of the Hebrew alphabet.

Ten beads of the series: Visualization: Old bearded king seen in profile. Name of the Sphere: **Kether (kaitair)**.

Closing

Visualize before you the triangle composed of the ten letters of the Tetragrammaton.

$$\begin{array}{ccccc} & & & & ׳ \\ & & ה & ׳ & \\ & ו & ה & ׳ & \\ ה & ו & ה & ׳ & \end{array}$$

Then pronounce the letters beginning by the bottom of the triangle:

Yod—He—Vav—He

Yod—He—Vav

Yod—He

Yod

Stay silent and receptive for a while, then stand up, put the prayer beads aside, and extinguish the candle saying:

May this light continue to shine in the depths of my being!

TWO-PERSON RITUAL

This ritual can be performed as a couple to 1. balance the invisible bodies, 2. rise on the planes, and 3. heal an individual. The process below includes these purposes. You can also decide to focus more on one purpose than the other. In this case, just update the dedication that is spoken at the beginning of the ritual.

Organization of the Place

One of the participants, the "receiver," will remain relaxed while the other will perform the ritual. The receiver will lie on his back in a relaxed position on a couch, yoga mat, carpet, massage table, etc. If possible, his body should be in the east-west direction, with his head to the east. The one who performs the ritual will adapt his position so that he can use the prayer beads with his left hand and keep his right hand free.

A circle can be placed around the two participants. You can draw it on the floor or use a white cord.

Light a candle and carefully put it inside the circle, to the east.

Process

1. Having the prayer beads in your left hand, describe the sphere, just as you did in the opening of the individual ritual. Then say:

> **May this ritual be dedicated to ...** *name of the receiver ...*
> **May he/she ascend to the divine planes in order to balance his/her body, access the highest level of consciousness, and maintain the benefits of this spiritual experience!**

Then pronounce the four mystical names of the sphere: Cholem Yesodoth, Ashim, Sandalphon, Adonai Malekh.

2. Move consecutively to the four directions (East, South, West, and North). In each direction, turn yourself to face the receiver, directing the palm of your right hand in his/her direction. Then, with your forefinger on the corresponding bead, assume the angelic figure without describing it. Extend your right arm toward the receiver, palm open, and vibrate the angelic name you are incarnating.

3. Stand near his left leg, facing him. With your finger on the first separating bead, you will vibrate the sacred name Yeshua while tracing the invocation pentagram toward the receiver. Then extend your right hand in his direction and follow the first decade, vibrating the first letter, Yod, ten times.

   Stand by the receiver's left arm and proceed in the same way.
   Continue close to the head, the right arm, and the right leg.

4. Stay in this position and extend your right arm with the palm of your right hand a few inches above the solar center of the receiver. With the beads in your left hand, move your finger to the separating bead and vibrate the twenty-two letters of the Hebrew alphabet.

   Move your right hand above the first sephirah, Malkuth (feet). Then declaim the sixth decade, vibrating the Hebrew name of the sphere.

   When this is done, move your right hand as you did above the solar center and vibrate the twenty-two letters of the Hebrew alphabet on the separating bead.

   Move your right hand above the second sephirah, Yesod (sex), and proceed as you did before.

Continue for all the centers and decades. (Hod: right hip; Netzach: left hip; Tiphareth: center of the chest; Geburah: right shoulder; Chesed: left shoulder; Binah: right temple; Chokmah: left temple; Kether: top of the head.)

5. When this is done, move to the head of the receiver, turning your back on the east. Put the palm of your right hand above his forehead and pronounce the ten letters of the Tetragrammaton.

Yod—He—Vav—He
Yod—He—Vav
Yod—He
Yod

Put your prayer beads aside. Put your hands on the sides of the recipient's head, palms toward his temples, then blow three times on his forehead while visualizing that he accesses the highest levels of consciousness.

6. You can now listen to light, peaceful music or remain in silence for a while. After a few minutes, say:

All is accomplished!
May the light of the divine plane stay in you always,
balancing and protecting you in all aspects of your life!
So mote it be!

7. Finally, extinguish the candle and dismiss the circle.

GROUP RITUAL

This ritual can be used in a group to increase the invisible power generated by the joint pronunciations and visualizations. When you begin the process in a group, one participant should be chosen as the leader.

The purposes for a group can be the same as for a couple: 1. balancing the invisible bodies, 2. rising on the planes, and 3. healing of an individual.

Organization of the Place

Chairs can be arranged in a circle facing the center. A representation of the engraving by H. Khunrath can be put on the floor in the center.

A circle can be placed around the participants. You can draw it on the floor or use a white cord.

Light a candle and carefully place it at the center of the circle, on the symbolic representation by H. Khunrath.

In the case of a healing ritual, adapt the place as follows:

1. If the healing ritual is for someone who is physically present, organize the place as in couple work. Then the group leader will perform in the same way as with a couple, but everyone in the circle will participate in the ritual pronunciations.

2. If the healing ritual is for someone who is not physically present, put that person's photo in the center of the representation of the engraving. The name and date of birth of that person should be written on the back of the photo.

Process

1. Holding the prayer beads in his left hand, the group leader declaims the intention of this ritual work:

For a healing ritual:

May this ritual be dedicated to ... *name of the receiver ...*

For a simple group ritual:

May this ritual be dedicated to ...
(Each participant pronounces his own name).

One or two of the previous declarations are followed by:

May he/she ascend to the divine planes in order to balance his/her bodies, access the highest level of consciousness, and maintain the benefits of this spiritual experience!

Then pronounce the four mystical names of the sphere: Cholem Yesodoth, Ashim, Sandalphon, Adonai Malekh.

2. The ritual continues as described for individual practice from the "Establishment of the Guardians."

Ritual of the 22 Keys

This ritual belongs to the tradition of the Christian Qabalah and is still used within the Kabbalistic Order of the Rose-Cross.

Purpose

Harmonization and exploration of the Qabalistic Tree of Life.

Description of the Prayer Beads

This set of prayer beads is composed of forty beads separated in four series of ten deep-blue beads. Between each series, there is a separating white bead. Traditionally, three white ribbons are attached to it. A pin or medal featuring the main symbol of the Kabbalistic Order of the Rose-Cross can be attached to these ribbons. Each one can have one of the names of the three Kabbalistic veils written on it: **Ain Soph Aur (aïn sof or)**, **Ain Soph, Ain**.

Symbolism, Numbers, and General Process

This set of prayer beads is structured on multiples of four. Each series of ten beads is related to the letter Yod (י), the first letter of the Tetragrammaton, and to the ten sephiroth of the Qabalistic Tree of Life. The four series of ten beads are related to the four worlds, four elements, and four Hebrew letters of the Tetragrammaton. The sum of these beads is forty, which represents the letter Mem (מ). Associated with the four (ד) separating beads, the final number of beads is forty-four, which corresponds to the Hebrew word "Mad" (מד).

The letter Mem can be related to an undifferentiated primitive liquid—chaos (Nun). This chaos is shaped by a potentiating creative act, which gives it order and form. In Hebrew, the first Mem is open, like the womb of the dark Mother (chaos)

awaiting fertilization (the potentiating act). This is the first letter of Maim: "water." In Hebrew this word is written with three
letters. Two letters Mem surround the letter iod. It signifies the
waters that have not yet separated from the primal water.

The permutation of the word Mad (מד) gives us a specific
meaning: Dam (דמ), the blood. We have to remember that
blood has been considered in the Qabalistic tradition as one
of the vehicles of the soul.

In this ritual, each series of ten beads is connected to the
paths of the Qabalistic Tree, which is composed of ten spheres,
connected by a complex web of paths. The Qabalistic schools
and magick Orders may differ in the number of paths and the
correspondences of each one. In the modern Western tradition,
there are two main ways to specify this: 1. a web of twenty-two
paths related to the twenty-two letters of the Hebrew Alphabet;
2. a web of twenty-four paths related to the twenty-four letters
of the Greek Alphabet. The Kabbalistic Order of the Rose-Cross
uses the first system. Don't worry about the correspondences
between the paths, the Hebrew letters, or other symbolic elements. This ritual can be used regardless of which system you
use. Just remember that you are directly connecting to the
source of this tradition: the sacred letters, which, according to
the Zohar, were used to build the cosmos.

Meditation

I provide you two meditations that are focused on two different purposes. However, you can also link the two series. In
this case, the first one must be followed by the second one.

The first one is intended to raise your consciousness to the highest level of the Qabalistic Tree following what is called the "path of the arrow."

The second meditation is intended to attract the divine power in your microcosm, following the same path.

(The tools for the meditation are optional. However, it is always better, if you can, to use at least a candle.)

Hang a representation of the engraving by H. Khunrath in front of you. In front of it, place a white or plain beeswax candle and the required prayer beads for this ritual.

Sit comfortably facing east, take your prayer beads, and breathe peacefully for a few minutes.

First Meditation

The sequence to be used for this first meditation is the following:

On each separating bead pronounce four times the sacred name **Ieouah (iaiooa)**.

On the series of ten beads proceed as explained below:

First series of ten beads (for Malkuth): **Relem Iezodot (kheuleum iaisodot)**

Second series of ten beads (for Yesod): **Keroubim (kairoobim)**

Third series of ten beads (for Tiphareth): **Ramael (*kh*maail)**

Fourth series of ten beads (for Kether): **Eeieh (aiaiiai)**

On the last separating bead (the first you began with) pronounce:

- **Ain Soph Aur** (aïn sof or)
- **Ain Soph**
- **Ain**

Breathe silently for few minutes without focusing on specific thoughts.

Then feel a spiritual light surrounding you, purifying all levels of your being.

Stay silent and receptive for a while, then stand up, put the prayer beads aside, and extinguish the candle, saying:

May this light continue to shine in the depths of my being!

Second Meditation

The sequence to be used for this second meditation is the following:

On the first separating bead, pronounce:

- **Ain**
- **Ain Soph**
- **Ain Soph Aur**

On each following separating bead pronounce four times the sacred name **Ieouah**. *(See pronunciations above.)*

On the series of ten beads proceed as explained below:

First series of ten beads (for Kether): **Eeieh**

Second series of ten beads (for Tiphareth): **Ramael**

Third series of ten beads (for Yesod): **Keroubim**

Fourth series of ten beads (for Malkuth): **Relem Iezodot**

On the last separating bead (the first you begin with) pronounce also four times the sacred name **Ieouah**.

Conclude the meditation in the same way you did for the first meditation with the same declamation.

INDIVIDUAL RITUAL
Tools

Hang a representation of the engraving by H. Khunrath in front of you. Put a candle (beeswax or white candle) in front of it, along with the specific prayer beads required for this ritual.

Opening

Light the candle. Holding the prayer beads in your left hand, touch the pin or the medal with your right forefinger. Close your eyes and relax for a few minutes. You may stand, sit on a chair, or find some other comfortable position.

Be aware of your body, your feet, and their contact with the ground. Breathe slowly and deeply as you gradually relax. Become aware of your body, what you hear, what you feel, etc. As you become more and more aware of your own being, distracting thoughts will progressively disappear.

Using the 22 Keys

Imagine that you are in a quiet and peaceful setting at night. Around you, the air is clear and crisp, and the sky is dark and starless. Mentally looking around, notice the double circle and the sphere in which you stand. Visualize yourself standing in the center of this space, whether or not you are actually standing.

The first decade: Put your thumb and forefinger on the first separating bead (next to the ribbons). Breathe slowly and vibrate the following sacred name four times: **Ieouah**.

Take the first bead of the first series as you did for the previous practices. Visualize before you the Hebrew letter **Tav** (ת). Try to keep the letter in your mind; take the second bead of this series and vibrate the same Hebrew letter again. Continue in the same way for the ten beads of this series.

The second decade: Put your thumb and forefinger on the second separating bead. Breathe slowly and vibrate the same sacred name four times: **Ieouah**.

Take the first bead of the second series as before. Visualize before you the Hebrew letter **Shin** (ש). Try to keep the letter in your mind as you vibrate the same Hebrew letter. Continue in the same way for the ten beads of this series.

From the third decade to the twenty-second decade: Proceed exactly in the same way for the other decades, keeping the four pronunciations of the sacred name **Ieouah** on each separating bead and the successive Hebrew letters for the other sets of ten beads.

The full succession of the other Hebrew letters you have to use is:

Decade 3: **Resh** (ר), Decade 4: **Qof** (ק), Decade 5: **Tsadi** (צ), Decade 6: **Pe** (פ), Decade 7: **Ayin** (ע), Decade 8: **Samekh** (ס), Decade 9: **Nun** (נ), Decade 10: **Mem** (מ), Decade 11: **Lamed** (ל), Decade 12: **Kaf** (כ), Decade 13: **Yod** (י), Decade 14: **Tet** (ט), Decade 15: **Het** (ח), Decade 16: **Zayin** (ז), Decade 17: **Vav** (ו), Decade 18: **He** (ה), Decade 19: **Dalet** (ד), Decade 20: **Gimel** (ג), Decade 21: **Bet** (ב), Decade 22: **Alef** (א).

Closing

When the entire series is done, put the three ribbons in your right hand, with your thumb and forefinger touching the medal or pin.

Visualize the three veils above your head. Pronounce successively the names of the three Qabalistic veils; at each name, visualize the veil opening.

1. **Ain Soph Aur**

2. **Ain Soph**

3. **Ain**

Breathe silently for few minutes, without focusing on specific thoughts.

Then feel a spiritual light surrounding you, purifying all levels of your being.

Stay silent and receptive for a while, then stand up, put the prayer beads aside, and extinguish the candle, saying:

May this light continue to shine in the depths of my being!

Two-person Ritual

This ritual can be used with a couple mainly for 1. exploring the Qabalistic Tree of Life, and 2. increasing the circulation of energy in your spiritual being. You may adapt the dedication if needed.

Organization of the Place

Organize the setting just like for a couple in the Ritual of the Blazing Wheel. One of the participants, the "receiver," will be relaxed while the other will perform the ritual for him.

Carefully light a candle and put it inside the circle, to the east.

Process

1. Taking the prayer beads in your right hand, stand at the receiver's head, facing west. Guide the receiver to visualize himself in a quiet and peaceful nighttime setting, where the air is clear and crisp. The sky above is dark and starless. You are standing at the center of this space. Then say:

> **May this ritual be dedicated to ...** *name of the receiver ...*
> **May the 22 keys open the sacred gates of the creation**
> **to increase the presence of the divine power inside the**
> **invisible bodies of ...** *name of the receiver ...* **!**

2. Direct your left hand toward the receiver. Keeping your hand in his direction, move counterclockwise around him in twenty-two consecutive steps. At each stop, begin with the separating bead and pronounce the Tetragrammaton **Ieouah**. Then vibrate the name of the letter ten times as you work with the ten beads in the series, as described in the individual version of this ritual. Use the order of letters below (reverse sequence):

Decade 1: **Tav** (ת); Decade 2: **Shin** (ש); Decade 3: **Resh** (ר); Decade 4: **Qof** (ק); Decade 5: **Tsadi** (צ); Decade 6: **Pe** (פ); Decade 7: **Ayin** (ע); Decade 8: **Samekh** (ס); Decade 9: **Nun** (נ); Decade 10: **Mem** (מ); Decade 11: **Lamed** (ל); Decade 12: **Kaf**

(כ); Decade 13: **Yod** (י); Decade 14: **Tet** (ט); Decade 15: **Het** (ח); Decade 16: **Zayin** (ז); Decade 17: **Vav** (ו); Decade 18: **He** (ה); Decade 19: **Dalet** (ד); Decade 20: **Gimel** (ג); Decade 21: **Bet** (ב); Decade 22: **Alef** (א).

3. When you are back, put the prayer beads in your left hand and take the three ribbons in your palm. Put your right hand above the receiver's forehead.

> Inhale and vibrate: **Ain Soph Aur.**
> Inhale and vibrate: **Ain Soph.**
> Inhale and vibrate: **Ain.**
> Remove your hand and blow three times on the receiver's head.

4. Direct your right hand toward the receiver. Keeping your hand in his direction, move clockwise around the receiver in twenty-two consecutive steps. With each step, work through the twenty-two decades as you did in step 2, but in the regular (forward) order of the letters:

Decade 1: **Alef** (א); Decade 2: **Bet** (ב); Decade 3: **Gimel** (ג); Decade 4: **Dalet** (ד); Decade 5: **He** (ה); Decade 6: **Vav** (ו); Decade 7: **Zayin** (ז); Decade 8: **Het** (ח); Decade 9: **Tet** (ט); Decade 10: **Yod** (י); Decade 11: **Kaf** (כ); Decade 12: **Lamed** (ל); Decade 13: **Mem** (מ); Decade 14: **Nun** (נ); Decade 15: **Samekh** (ס); Decade 16: **Ayin** (ע); Decade 17: **Pe** (פ); Decade 18: **Tsadi** (צ); Decade 19: **Qof** (ק); Decade 20: **Resh** (ר); Decade 21: **Shin** (ש); Decade 22: **Tav** (ת).

5. Put your prayer beads aside. Put your hands on the sides of the recipient's head, palms in the direction of his temples.

> Inhale and vibrate: **Ain Soph Aur**.
>
> Inhale and vibrate: **Ain Soph**.
>
> Inhale and vibrate: **Ain**.
>
> Then blow three times on his forehead while visualizing him accessing the highest levels of consciousness.

6. You can now play light, peaceful music or stay in silence for a while. After a few minutes, say:

> **All is accomplished!**
> **May the opening of the twenty-two sacred gates**
> **of the creation maintain the presence of the divine**
> **power inside your invisible bodies.**
> **May the light of the divine plane stay in you,**
> **always balancing and protecting you in all aspects**
> **of your life! So mote it be!**

7. Extinguish the candle and dismiss the circle.

GROUP RITUAL

The group practice can be used to 1. build and increase the egregore of a group; 2. increase the inner power of the macrocosm of all people present; and 3. increase the understanding of Hebrew Qabalah.

Organization of the Place

Organize the space as for the Ritual of the Blazing Wheel.

Process

1. Having the prayer beads in his left hand, the group leader declaims the intention of this ritual work:

May the opening of twenty-two sacred gates of the creation ... *name the intention of the ritual ...* **!**

2. The ritual continues using the following sequence, with the leader using the prayer beads just as for the individual and two-person rituals:

a) Vibrate ten decades from Tav to Aleph.

b) Vibrate the three names of the three veils.

c) Vibrate the ten decades from Aleph to Tav.

Ritual of the Tree of Life

The Qabalistic Tree of Life is one of the fundamental symbols of the Hebrew Qabalah and is also widely used in the Western magical tradition.

Purpose: This ritual will use the powers of the upper world of Atziluth to balance your inner being. This ritual should be performed after doing the previous Ritual of the 22 Keys.

Description of the Prayer Beads

The prayer beads used here are the same as for the Ritual of the 22 Keys, composed of forty-four beads.

Symbolism, Numbers, and General Process

The vibrations used in this ritual are the sacred names (in Atziluth) associated with the Hebrew letters as indicated in the chart below. As you can see, some names are repeated several times. This is normal.

El (ail): Corresponds to the Letter Mem

Ieouah (iaiooa): Letter Alef

Elohim (ailohim): Letter Shin

Elohim Tzebaoth (ailohim tsaibaot also **tsaivaot)**: Letter Bet

Elohim Gibor (ailohim gibor): Letter Pe

El (ail): Letter Kaf

IeouahTzebaoth (iaiooa tsaibaot): Letter Dalet

El Rai (ail khaï): Letter Gimel

Ieouah Elohim (iaiooa ailohim): Letter Tav

Aloah VaDaath (ailoa veudaat): Letter Resh

Elohim Gibor: Letter He

IeouahTzebaoth: Letter Vav

Elohim Tzebaoth: Letter Zayin

Chadai (chadaï): Letter Het

Eloha (ailoa): Letter Tet

Elohim Tzabaoth: Letter Yod

IeouahTzabaoth: Letter Lamed

Elohim Gibor: Letter Nun

El: Letter Samekh

Ieouah Elohim: Letter Ayin

Iaou (iaoo): Letter Tsadi

El: Letter Qof

The invocation of the divine names will be repeated ten times each.

Meditation

The sequence of this meditation must follow the Hebrew alphabet. This meditation is based on two of the main Qabalistic books, the *Sepher Yetzirah* and the *Zohar*. Both books explain clearly that God created the cosmos by the use of the twenty-two letters. According the Hebrew Qabalists, a meditation and pronunciation of these letters put your soul in this process. The energy with which you will be tuned will help you to a deeper understanding of these mysteries, and harmonize your psyche with the highest energies of the cosmos. This is a simple and very efficient process. The use of prayer beads is perfect for that.

(As usual the tools for the meditation are optional. However, it is always better, if you can, to use at least a candle.)

Hang a representation of the Qabalistic Tree of Life in front of you. Place three candles (beeswax or white candle) and the prayer beads in front of it.

Sit comfortably facing East, take your prayer beads, and breathe peacefully for a few minutes.

On every separating bead declaim the divine name **Ieouah.**

The series of ten beads must follow the letters of the Hebrew alphabet according the following list: **Mem, Alef, Shin, Bet, Pe, Kaf, Dalet, Gimel, Tav, Resh, He, Vav, Zayin, Het, Tet, Yod, Lamed, Nun, Samekh, Ayin, Tsadi, Qof.**

Each letter is pronounced ten times, one for each bead of the series.

When this is done, breathe silently for few minutes, with no specific thoughts.

Then feel a spiritual light surrounding you, purifying all the levels of your being.

Stay silent and receptive for a while, then stand, put the prayer beads aside, and extinguish the candles, saying:

May this light continue to shine in the depths of my being.

Individual Ritual

Tools

Hang a representation of the Qabalistic Tree of Life in front of you. Place three candles (beeswax or white candles) and the prayer beads in front of it.

Opening

Light the candle. Take the prayer beads as you did in the previous ritual and proceed.

Sequences of the Ritual

You may begin by vibrating ten times (on the first series of ten beads) the divine name of the letter Mem: **El**. Then, continue in the same way for the twenty-one other names, corresponding the letters to the divine names in the above list. It is important to keep a correct sequence of vibrations at a moderate speed in order to begin a kind of active meditation.

When this is done, conclude with the following sentence:

Then Ieouah Elohim (iaiooa ailohim) formed man of the dust of the ground, and breathed into his nostrils the breath of life; and man became a living soul. [15]

Closing

Breathe silently for few minutes, with no specific thoughts.

Then feel a spiritual light surrounding you, purifying all the levels of your being.

Stay silent and receptive for a while, then stand, put the prayer beads aside, and extinguish the candles, saying:

May this light continue to shine in the depths of my being!

TWO-PERSON RITUAL

This ritual can be used for a couple for the same purposes as the individual ritual. It is a powerful way to magically intensify each aspect of the inner Tree of Life.

Organization of the Place

Before performing this ritual you have to prepare two sets of printouts: 1. the twenty-two Hebrew letters, and 2. the Qabalistic seals of the spheres. [16]

Hang a representation of the Qabalistic Tree of Life in front of you with three candles (beeswax or white candles) in front of it.

---

15. Bible, Genesis 2:7.
16. You can download the files of the Qabalistic seals of the spheres from the Aurum Solis website (www.aurumsolis.info) or order them online already printed on vinyl.

As in the ritual of the Blazing Wheel, the receiver lies on his back in a relaxed position. He can be on a couch, yoga mat, carpet, massage table, etc. If possible, position the receiver's body in the east-west direction, with his head toward the east. Then, put each seal of the spheres between the correct position on his body and the floor. You can find these positions in the chart of the seals.

Next, put the Hebrew letters upon his body. Since the correspondences between the paths of the Qabalistic Tree and the Hebrew letters may vary according to different traditions, choose the system of your own school or tradition.

Process

1. Light the candles and stand by the receiver's head. Put the palms of both hands upon his head, saying:

May the divine power of the sphere of Atziluth balance the inner being of ... *name of the receiver ...*

2. Holding the prayer beads in your left hand, go near the letter Mem, facing the receiver. Extend your right hand upon the letter Mem and vibrate ten times (on the first series of ten beads) the divine name of this letter: **El.**

3. Continue in the same way for the following twenty-one letters.

4. When this is done, conclude with the following sentence:

Then Ieouah Elohim (iaiooa ailohim) formed man of the dust of the ground, and breathed into his nostrils the breath of life; and man became a living soul.[17]

Blow on the receiver's chest four times and remain silent for a while.

5. Extinguish the candles, saying:

**May this light continue to shine
in the depths of your being!
So mote it be!**

Group Ritual

The purpose in a group is the same as for a couple. The only difference is the increased effect of the energy generated by the group.

Organization of the Place and Process

Organize the space as you would for a couple. The participants' chairs are lined up in two lines parallel to the receiver and oriented east-west. One participant is chosen to proceed just as in the ritual practice for the couple. Everyone will vibrate the sacred names at the same time.

The sentence of closing is read only by the one acting on the person for whom the group is working.

---

17. Bible, Genesis 2:7.

Ritual of the Nine Choirs of Angels

The use of these prayer beads has a unique background story. According the story, in 1751 the Archangel Michael appeared to a Portuguese nun, Antonia d'Astonac. "I want," said the archangel, "that you recite in my honor and in union with the nine choirs of the angels, nine times one Pater and three Ave's. You will achieve these salutations by four Pater's: the first one to honor me, the second to honor the Archangel Gabriel, the third for Raphael, and the last one for the guardian angel." He promised to give protection to those who use these prayers. From this revelation, a specific set of prayer beads named for Michael was created. A few years later, a guild called "Archiconfrérie de Saint Michel," was created on the famous French island Mont Saint-Michel.

In the 1980s, the Guild of Michael was nearly unknown. I had the good fortune to meet the head of the Guild in a vaulted room of the monastery in the extraordinary city of Brittany, built on the island in the northwest of France. After a fascinating conversation, I accepted the gift of a set of prayer beads and the membership card of the Guild. The Guild's head's considerate sharing of what was important to him was gladly welcomed at that particular point in my life.

A few years later, when I was introduced in the Kabbalistic Order of the Rose-Cross, I discovered a more esoteric way to use the prayer beads. The members of this Order know how to use them without the Catholic connection.

Description of the Prayer Beads

This set of prayer beads is composed of nine series of three beads separated by a separating bead. The string with a medal or symbol attached has four beads. In the Kabbalistic Order of the Rose-Cross, the medal depicts the nine choirs of angels in relation to the God of this tradition.

When possible, the color of the beads can follow the traditional Qabalistic colors provided in the hierarchies of the angels.

Symbolism, Numbers, and General Process
The Four Archangels

The four archangels are associated below with their description and various indications that are useful for your practice.

Raphael: He has two pristine white wings and wears a long green-gray robe. In one hand he carries a little box made of wood, ivory, and precious metal. His other hand holds the hand of a young child carrying a big fish: Direction East, from dawn to noon, in charge of healing and purification.

Haniel: He has two pristine white wings and is wearing a long pink robe. He carries white roses in his arms: Direction South, from dusk to midnight, associated with intellectual activity.

Gabriel: He has two pristine white wings and wears a bluish-white robe. He holds a ruby-red lamp in one hand: Direction West, from midnight to dawn, chief of the celestial army, associated with knowledge and bravery.

Michael: He has two pristine white wings and is wearing a long white-golden dress. He holds a palm in one hand and a white flag with a red cross in the other. A dragon is next to him: Direction North, from noon to dusk, he is the other chief of the celestial army.

The Hierarchies of the Angels

The hierarchies of angels are associated below with their color and various indications that are useful for your practice.

Chaioth Ha Qadesh (khaiot hakodaich): Holy Living Ones, shimmering white. This is the upper level in the system of the Hebrew Qabalah. These Beings give and divide up the principle of life that allows human beings to progress toward the divine unity. They provide enlightenment.

They are symbolically represented by a quadruple figure composed of a lion, a bull, an eagle, and a man.

Auphanim (ofanim): Wheels, billowing blue-black. The Wheels are angels of justice carrying orders from God. Their functions are to balance and adjust the chaotic powers. They give to humans the light of the mind and the power of wisdom.

Aralim (aralim): The Thrones, soft red-brown. They give the power to meet and to build together.

Chasmalim (khachmalim): Shining Ones, light royal blue. They are the origin of the energy, power, and light that give humans inner strength, allowing them to defeat their inner enemies and to reach their goals.

Seraphim (sairafim): Burning Ones, fiery red. They produce the four subtle elements: Fire, Air, Water, and Earth. They support human beings against the enemies external to their physical body. They are the angels of love, light, and fire.

Malachim (malakhim): The Kings, pale golden yellow. The Kings give power to defeat the powers of deception and give to humans the reward for their efforts.

Elohim (ailohim): The Gods, light turquoise. They allow human beings dominion over living beings.

Beni Elohim (bnaï ailohim): Sons of the Gods, light apricot. They allow human beings dominion over animals.

Cheroubim (kairoobim): The Powerful, lavender. They guide human beings to the eternal life. They are the guardians of the entrance of heaven.

Meditation

(Use the same tools and proceed as you did for the Ritual for the Blazing Wheel. Remember that these tools are optional for the meditation. However, it is always better, if you can, to use at least a candle.)

Sit comfortably facing east, take your prayer beads, and breathe peacefully for a few minutes.

Use successively the four separating beads that are on the string outside the circle.

On the first bead, say:

In front of me, in the East, I invoke you, Raphael (Rafaail)!

On the second bead, say:

At my right, in the South, I invoke you, Haniel (Haniail)!

On the third bead, say:

Behind me, in the West, I invoke you, Gabriel (Gabriail)!

On the fourth bead, say:

At my left, in the North, I invoke you, Michael
(Mi*kh*aail)!

Now use the other beads that are in the circle. On each separating bead pronounce three times the sacred name **Ieouah**.

On the series of three beads, pronounce successively the following sacred names of the archangels (three times on each bead). You can find the pronunciations of the names in the previous paragraph. This first cycle of the meditation will be the ascent to the highest level.

1. Cheroubim

2. Beni Elohim

3. Elohim

4. Malachim

5. Seraphim

6. Chasmalim

7. Aralim

8. Auphanim

9. Chaioth Ha Qadesh

This second cycle of the meditation is the descent from the highest level in order to give you the blessing of the archangelic choirs.

1. Chaioth Ha Qadesh

2. Auphanim

3. Aralim

4. Chasmalim

5. Seraphim

6. Malachim

7. Elohim

8. Beni Elohim

9. Cheroubim

Stay silent and receptive for a while, then stand up, put the prayer beads aside, and extinguish the candle, saying:

**May this light continue to shine
in the depths of my being!**

First Individual Ritual—
Descent of the Celestial Power

Process

There are two ways to use these prayer beads: 1. to ascend to the divine, and 2. to invoke the celestial powers to descend to us. Consequently, the way to invoke the choirs of the angels will be different in each case, beginning at the top (Chaioth Ha Qadesh) or bottom (Cheroubim).

I will now precisely explain these two processes, giving you a few descriptions to visualize. Remember that you do not have to visualize everything at the beginning. These two processes can be used with only the vibrations of the sacred names. They are powerful enough to give you the full benefits of this ritual.

The Foundation

Proceed as you did for the Ritual for the Blazing Wheel (i.e., the visualization of the circle and the sphere).

When this is done, pronounce the four sacred names:

Cholem Yesodoth (kheuleum iaisodot)

Ashim (achim)

Sandalphon (sandalfon)

Adonai Malekh (adonaï meuleu*kh*)

Stay silent for a while, feeling the presences all around you. Imagine that you are raising your head to look above (without moving your physical head). Visualize at a distance a sphere of violet. Focus your attention on it and vibrate the sacred name **Shaddai El Chai** (chadaï ail khaï).

Now you are surrounded by the violet light.

With your spiritual vision still focused on the upper levels, you can now see a yellow sphere. Visualize yourself ascending slightly in its direction without reaching it.

The Establishment of the Guardians

The Four Beads

Proceed with the four beads that are on the separated string in the same way you did in the Ritual for the Blazing Wheel.

The Ascent

Above you shines a yellow sphere. Imagine yourself becoming lighter and lighter, rising toward it. The pure yellow light surrounds you. Vibrate the sacred name **Raphael**. Remain silent for a few seconds, focusing on the surrounding light.

Then visualize a sphere of intense white light above you and rise toward it until you are inside it.

Above this sphere, you see three rippling veils, through which you glimpse a spiritual light. Keeping your focus on these visualizations, pronounce the following invocation:

> **I ... *say your name* ... I invoke the spiritual power, origin of everything. Sacred Fire, soul of the universe, Eternal principle of the world and beings, hear my voice.**
>
> **My desire is pure and I aspire to the enlightenment of my being so that my work can be accomplished.**
>
> **May you at this moment send a ray of your divine power so that each angelic choir will assist me in carrying out this work of my being.**
>
> **So mote it be!**

Then vibrate the following divine names:

> **Eheieh** (aiaiiai)
>
> **Metatron** (maitatron)

Next, proceed to the invocation of the angelic choirs according to the following process.

Descent of the Light

1. Chaioth Ha Qadesh (khaiot hakodaich)

Take the first bead between the thumb and forefinger of your right hand. Breathe and take the time to build your visualization. You have two choices here: 1. visualize only the colored light; 2. visualize the full picture. Choose according to your level of practice, then progressively challenge yourself and go forward with a more complete visualization. You can also use a recording to guide you during these visualizations. You will be provided for each choir (a) the color, and (b) the full description. Use whichever is most appropriate for you.

a) Color: Shimmering white

b) Description: Visualize four lights around you, each placed on a hill in one of the four directions. The light to the east (in front of you) is yellow, to the south (on your right) is red, to the west (behind you) is white, and to the north (on your left) is black.

These lights glow like fires from which appear the four figures of the "Holy Living Beings." In front of you is the eagle; the lion is on your right; the man dressed in white, behind you; and on your left, the bull. These beings radiate a divine and serene power. Their energy and light penetrate your body. A rustling sound surrounds you, like the sound of water or insect wings. Your whole being is filled with strength. With your fingers still on the same separating bead, declaim:

O Chaioth Ha Qadesh, I invoke you. May the manifestation of your presence inflame all the levels of my being, increasing in me the quality of charity.

Then pronounce the sacred name of the choir one time on each of the three following beads.

2. Auphanim (ofanim)

As you did for the first choir, take the next separating bead between your right thumb and forefinger. Breathe and take the time to build your visualization.

a) Color: Billowing blue-black

b) Description: Huge wheels of fire surround the throne of God. They are covered with eyes and their color is like polished copper. They turn on themselves and flames escape from their circumference, emitting a characteristic whistle. An omnipresent voice seems to speak to you from within. A warm breath spreads in the air like heat waves. Above you shines a firmament with the appearance of a crystal. Beside you and larger than the wheels are beings dressed in shining white. They seem to surround the wheels with their large wings. Two wings surround their bodies and two more wings extend in the back.

With your fingers still on the separating bead, declaim:

O Auphanim, I invoke you. May the manifestation of your presence inflame all the levels of my being, helping me to destroy vice and increase the virtues.

Then pronounce the sacred name of the choir, once on each of the three following beads.

3. Aralim (aralim)

As you did for the first choir, take the separating bead between your right thumb and forefinger. Breathe and take the time to build your visualization.

a) Color: Soft red-brown

b) Description: These spiritual beings have a color of gray granite. They are wiry, with long faces. They sit on thrones in a profound silence, giving a sense of great serenity. Silence reigns over the scene.

With your fingers on the separating bead, declaim:

O Aralim, I invoke you. May the manifest station of your presence inflame all the levels of my being, helping me to build a true and sincere friendship.

Then pronounce the sacred name of the choir, once on each of the three following beads.

4. Chasmalim (khachmalim)

Once again, take the next separating bead between your right thumb and forefinger. Breathe and take the time to build your visualization.

a) Color: Light royal blue

b) Description: These beings wear robes reaching their feet. They wear a gold belt and green sandals. In their right hand, they carry a golden wand throwing lightning; and in the left, a divine seal. Sometimes they carry a golden orb or a scepter. The ground on which they stand is made of slate and has multiple symbolic signs of light color.

With your fingers still on the separating bead, declaim:

O Chasmalim, I invoke you. May the manifestation of your presence inflame all the levels of my being, helping me to find the right balance between the world in which I live, and myself.

Then pronounce the sacred name of the choir, once on each of the three following beads.

5. Seraphim (sairafim)

Again, take the next separating bead between your right thumb and forefinger. Breathe and take the time to build your visualization.

a) **Color**: Fiery red

b) **Description**: Around you shines an incandescent white light. The Seraphim fly above the throne of God, constantly singing his praises. This song fills this divine place and resonates through you. Their six wings glimmer with a thousand colors. Two wings cover their faces, two cover their feet, and two allow them to fly. Their bodies are a pure stream of light, undulating like the body of a snake. They emit flames that warm up the entire atmosphere. They each carry a wand of burnished copper in their right hand.

With your fingers still on the separating bead, declaim:

> **O Seraphim, I invoke you. May the manifestation of
> your presence inflame all the levels of my being, help-
> ing me to find inner peace.**

Then pronounce the sacred name of the choir, once on each
of the three following beads.

6. Malachim (malakhim)

Again, take the next separating bead between your right
thumb and forefinger. Breathe and take the time to build your
visualization.

a) Color: Pale golden yellow

b) Description: Seven kings sit on golden thrones that
form a semicircle on a red rocky surface in a seemingly de-
serted area. Several steps allow the visitor to reach their level.
The sky is clear blue, illuminated by bright lightning spring-
ing from the kings' crowns. Each king carries a crystal cup
containing a purple liquid.

With your fingers still on the separating bead, declaim:

> **O Malachim, I invoke you. May the manifestation of
> your presence inflame all the levels of my being, help-
> ing me to attain inner freedom.**

Then pronounce the sacred name of the choir, once on each
of the three following beads.

7. Elohim (ailohim)

Again, take the next separating bead between your right thumb and forefinger. Breathe and take the time to build your visualization.

a) **Color**: Light turquoise

b) **Description**: The sky is filled with an intense blue light. Several beings dressed in white linen stand on the top of a green hill. A golden color strongly radiates from their faces, and their eyes seem to emit flames. They appear to be brilliant suns.

With your fingers on the separating bead, declaim:

O Elohim, I invoke you. May the manifestation of your presence inflame all the levels of my being, helping me to discover and achieve my inner Great Work.

Then pronounce the sacred name of the choir, once on each of the three following beads.

8. Beni Elohim (bnaï ailohim)

Again, take the next separating bead between your right thumb and forefinger. Breathe and take the time to build your visualization.

a) **Color**: Light apricot

b) **Description**: Before you is a starry sky over a dark sea. Sparks of fire illuminate the surface of the sea and appear to move over it like waves. Each movement is accompanied by a sound: a voice that seems to retreat, then approach us.

With your fingers on the separating bead, declaim:

O Beni Elohim, I invoke you. May the manifestation of your presence inflame all the levels of my being, helping me to maintain a pure moral honesty.

Then pronounce the sacred name of the choir, once on each of the three following beads.

9. Cheroubim (kairoobim)

Again, take the next separating bead between your right thumb and forefinger. Breathe and take the time to build your visualization.

a) **Color**: Lavender

b) **Description**: Before you is the Garden of Eden. Armed with a flaming sword, the four-winged Cheroubim guard the entrance. No one can reach this place without being interrogated by these two guards. Above, far into the bright light of heaven, other Cheroubim surround the throne of God.

With your fingers on the separating bead, declaim:

O Cheroubim, I invoke you. May the manifestation of your presence inflame all the levels of my being, surrounding it by a beneficial protection.

Then pronounce the sacred name of the choir, once on each of the three following beads.

Closing

Put the prayer beads aside and cross your arms upon your chest, left forearm upon right forearm, so that their junction is at the center of your chest.

Stay silent and receptive for a while, then stand up, put the prayer beads aside, and extinguish the candle, saying:

The rite is accomplished!
May this light continue to shine
in the depths of my being!

Second Individual Ritual—
Ascent through the Angelic Choirs
The Establishment of the Guardians

Proceed as you did in the previous ritual for "The Establishment of the Guardians."

The Ascent

1. Cheroubim

Take the first bead between your right thumb and forefinger. Visualize a lavender sphere above you. Breathe peacefully and pronounce the name of the sphere: **Levanah** (laivana). As you pronounce the name of the sphere, imagine yourself rising into the air until you are at the center of it, feeling its color all around you.

Then vibrate the divine name **Shaddai El Chai** (chadaï ail khaï)

During this pronunciation, the color intensifies. Breathe, relax, and take the time to build your visualization. You have two choices here: 1. Continue to intensify the colored light; 2. Visualize the full picture of the Cheroubim. Choose according to your level of practice and memorization. Then, as previously, challenge yourself and go forward with a more complete visualization.

With your fingers still on the same separating bead, declaim:

O Cheroubim, I invoke you. May the manifestation of your presence inflame all the levels of my being, surrounding it by a beneficial protection.

Then pronounce the sacred name of this choir, once on each of the three following beads.

2. Beni Elohim

Again, take the separating bead between your right thumb and forefinger. Breathe and visualize, at a distance, a sphere colored **light apricot**.

Breathe peacefully and pronounce the name of the sphere: **Kokab** (ko*kh*ab).

While you pronounce the name of the sphere, imagine yourself rising into the air until you are at the center of it, feeling its color all around you.

Then vibrate the divine name **Elohim Tzabaoth** (ailohim tsaibaot).

Continue to intensify the color or visualize the choir of angels according to the previous description.

With your fingers on the separating bead, declaim:

O Beni Elohim, I invoke you. May the manifestation of your presence inflame all the levels of my being, helping me to maintain a pure moral honesty.

Then pronounce the sacred name of the choir, once on each of the three following beads.

3. Elohim

Again, take the separating bead between your right thumb and forefinger. Breathe and visualize, at a distance, a sphere colored **light turquoise**.

Breathe peacefully and pronounce the name of the sphere: **Nogah** (noga).

While you pronounce the name of the sphere, imagine yourself rising into the air until you are at the center of it, feeling its color all around you.

Then vibrate the divine name **Ieouah Tzabaoth** (iaiooa tsaibaot).

Continue to intensify the color or visualize the choir of angels according to the previous description.

With your fingers still on the same separating bead, declaim:

O Elohim, I invoke you. May the manifestation of your presence inflame all the levels of my being, helping me to discover and achieve my inner Great Work.

Then pronounce the sacred name of the choir, once on each of the three following beads.

4. Malachim

Again, take the separating bead between your right thumb and forefinger. Breathe and visualize, at a distance, a sphere colored **pale golden yellow**.

Breathe peacefully and pronounce the name of the sphere: **Shemesh** (chaimaich).

While you pronounce the name of the sphere, imagine yourself rising into the air until you are at the center of it, feeling its color all around you.

Then vibrate the divine name **Ieouah Aloah VaDaath** (iaiooa ailoa veudaat).

Continue to intensify the color or visualize the choir of angels according to the previous description.

With your fingers still on the same separating bead, declaim:

O Malachim, I invoke you. May the manifestation of your presence inflame all the levels of my being, helping me to attain inner freedom.

Then pronounce the sacred name of the choir, once on each of the three following beads.

5. Seraphim

Again, take the separating bead between your right thumb and forefinger. Breathe and visualize, at a distance, a sphere colored **fiery red**.

Breathe peacefully and pronounce the name of the sphere: **Madim** (madim).

While you pronounce the name of the sphere, imagine yourself rising into the air until you are at the center of it, feeling its color all around you.

Then vibrate the divine name **Elohim Gibor** (ailohim gibor).

Continue to intensify the color or visualize the choir of angels according to the previous description.

O Seraphim, I invoke you. May the manifestation of your presence inflame all the levels of my being, helping me to find inner peace.

Then pronounce the sacred name of the choir, once on each of the three following beads.

6. Chasmalim

Again, take the separating bead between your right thumb and forefinger. Breathe and visualize, at a distance, a sphere colored **light royal blue**.

Breathe peacefully and pronounce the name of the sphere: **Tzedek** (tsaidaik).

While you pronounce the name of the sphere, imagine yourself rising into the air until you are at the center of it, feeling its color all around you.

Then vibrate the divine name **El** (ail).

Continue to intensify the color or visualize the choir of angels according to the previous description.

With your fingers still on the same separating bead, declaim:

O Chasmalim, I invoke you. May the manifestation of your presence inflame all the levels of my being, helping me to find the right balance between the world in which I live and myself.

Then pronounce the sacred name of the choir, once on each of the three following beads.

7. Aralim

Again, take the separating bead between your right thumb and forefinger. Breathe and visualize, at a distance, a sphere colored **soft red-brown**.

Breathe peacefully and pronounce the name of the sphere: **Shabbathai** (chabataï).

While you pronounce the name of the sphere, imagine yourself rising into the air until you are at the center of it, feeling its color all around you.

Then vibrate the divine name **Ieouah Elohim** (iaiooa ailo-him).

Continue to intensify the color or visualize the choir of angels according to the previous description.

With your fingers still on the same separating bead, de-claim:

O Aralim, I invoke you. May the manifestation of your presence inflame all the levels of my being, helping me to build true and sincere friendship.

Then pronounce the sacred name of the choir, once on each of the three following beads.

8. Auphanim

Again, take the separating bead between your right thumb and forefinger. Breathe and visualize, at a distance, a sphere colored **billowing blue-black**.

Breathe peacefully and pronounce the name of the sphere: **Mazlot** (mazlot).

While you pronounce the name of the sphere, imagine yourself rising into the air until you are at the center of it, feeling its color all around you.

Then vibrate the divine name **Iah** (ia).

Continue to intensify the color or visualize the choir of angels according to the previous description.

With your fingers still on the same separating bead, declaim:

O Auphanim, I invoke you. May the manifestation of your presence inflame all the levels of my being, helping me to destroy vice and increase virtues.

Then pronounce the sacred name of the choir, once on each of the three following beads.

9. Chaioth Ha Qadesh
Again, take theseparating bead between your right thumb and forefinger. Breathe and visualize, at a distance, a sphere colored **shimmering white**.

Breathe peacefully and pronounce the name of the sphere: **Rashith Ha Gilgalim** (rachit hagilgalim).

While you pronounce the name of the sphere, imagine yourself rising into the air until you are at the center of it, feeling its color all around you.

Then vibrate the divine name **Eheieh** (aiaiiai).

Continue to intensify the color or visualize the choir of angels according to the previous description.

With your fingers still on the same separating bead, declaim:

> **O Chaioth Ha Qadesh, I invoke you. May the manifestation of your presence inflame all the levels of my being, increasing in me the quality of charity.**

Then pronounce the sacred name of the choir, once on each of the three following beads.

Above you are the three mysterious veils. Beyond them, you can feel the presence of a spiritual life. Focusing on this divine presence, declaim:

> **I ... *say your name* ... invoke the spiritual power, origin of everything. Sacred Fire, soul of the universe, Eternal principle of the world and beings, listen to my words.**

> **My desire is pure and I aspire to the enlightenment of my being so that my work can be accomplished.**

> **May you at this time send a ray of your divine power to help in the evolution of my being.**

> **So mote it be!**

Visualize a light coming through the veils, descending upon you and penetrating your entire being.

Closing

Take the string with your left hand and grab the medal between your right thumb and forefinger. Close your eyes for a few minutes and relax.

After a few moments, visualize that you are the center of the double circle in the sphere of Malkuth. It is quiet and peaceful. This double sphere is filled with the seven colors of the rainbow, which shimmer and sparkle peacefully around you.

Then vibrate the mystical following name:

Cholem Yesodoth (kholeum iaisodot)

Stay silent for a few moments, simply feeling the presence of the divine powers of the sphere in which you stand.

Put the prayer beads aside and cross your arms upon your chest, left forearm upon right forearm, so that their junction is at the center of your chest.

Stay silent and receptive for a while, then stand up, put the prayer beads aside, and extinguish the candle, saying:

The rite is accomplished!
May this light continue to shine
in the depths of my being!

Two-person Ritual

This ritual is used for the same purpose of the individual practice: 1. raising your consciousness on the highest levels with the assistance of the choirs of angels, and 2. receiving the virtues provided by each choir.

You can use it to ascend or to invite the divine power.

Organization of the Place

Using the same prayer beads, you will practice this ritual together, seated on chairs facing each other. Hold the prayer beads in your right hand and take your partner's left hand with your left hand. You will maintain this contact during the ritual.

Process

For maximum efficiency, both of you should have already practiced the individual ritual.

The visualizations are not required during this practice. The vibrations of the sacred names you will use are enough to reactivate the connection you have already created during your individual practice. Try to follow a regular, moderate rhythm of vibrations of the names. One person should be chosen to read the intentions to each angel choir. Depending on the intention of the practice, you may decide not to pronounce the intentions associated with the choirs of angels. In this case, pronounce the vibrations of each choir four times instead of three.

If visions occur, welcome them but do not focus on them.

The sequences of sacred names used are the same as in the previous meditation.

GROUP RITUAL

Proceed exactly in the same way for a group as for the two-person ritual.

Organization of the Place and Process

Organize the chairs in a circle, facing the center. With the beads in your right hand, put your left hand on the right forearm (or thigh) of the person on your left. Obviously, you must be close to each other in order to create a real circle. This chain will be a powerful tool to increase the efficiency of this ritual practice.

Chapter 5

Hermetic Tradition

Surprisingly, the God Hermes is better known than Hermetism,[18] even though this tradition shaped most of what is known today as the Western initiatic tradition.

Hermetism comes from the ancient Egyptian city of Hermopolis. It is there that the clergy of the powerful God Thoth created a tradition emphasized in Alexandria during the first century BCE.

Rooted on pre-Christian philosophy and religious beliefs, an inspiring tradition was given birth by a group of adepts using the revelations of Hermes contained in the books *Chaldaean Oracles* and *Corpus Hermeticum*.[19] These collections of writings were considered sacred. Some of these texts emphasized the philosophical part. The adepts using these books were eventually known as Neoplatonicians. They unified the spiritual platonic tradition and the heritage of Hermes. Others developed the magical and Theurgic dimension and gave birth to Theurgy.

---

18. Sometimes spelled "Hermeticism."
19. Also referred to as the "Hermetica."

Hermetic prayer beads are Theurgic (magical) tools developed in the Ordo Aurum Solis to work ritually on mantras and respiration. The Hermetic Pagan system used for 3,000 years remains the blueprint that structures the ritual practices.

Ritual of the Circled Cross

This first ritual is associated with a representation that has been used in the Hermetic tradition since the Renaissance period and presumably earlier. This representation is known as the "circled cross." I already spoke about the Christian Qabalah and its relation with the symbol of the rose. Obviously, various ritual representations have been used in past centuries to speak about the deep symbolism of this mysterious flower. Dante was one initiate who placed the rose at the heart of his mystical book *The Divine Comedy*. The earliest symbolism of the Rose-Cross tradition put a cross in the center of a rose, not vice versa. Progressively, this symbolic rose was simplified in the Hermetic groups and became a simple circle surrounding an equal-armed cross. Sometime in the past, the symbol of the double square was associated with this circled cross.[20]

The correspondences of the equal-armed cross are deeply connected to the four directions and the elements. However, the Hermetists associate this symbol with three principles: feminine, male, and androgynous. These three aspects can be found in each of us and must be balanced on the spiritual and material levels in order to provide a good life.

At the same time and on the magical level, this figure acts as a healing sign capable of protecting you. I have used it sev-

---

20. You can see a picture of this on my website: www.debiasi.org.

eral times in this way and it is interesting to see the effect of this sign on one's aura.

I remember speaking with an old woman who explained to me that she was feeling more and more oppressed every day. She described symptoms identical to a physical suffocation, but on a spiritual level. We meditated together, and I began the occult process of seeing her aura. I was surprised to see a kind of solid surface confining the shining lights of her aura. Too much focused on the desire to be protected, she had created a barrier that now suffocated her. The only and simple thing to do was use the circled cross to open this Hermetic envelope around her aura and place a balanced protection capable of filtering the natural circulation of energy. As I will show you below in the use of this ritual, I used this seal and invocations in the four directions of her aura. The effect was immediate and she began to breathe more deeply and feel more relaxed. The result of this energetic work was permanent, and she never again felt this kind of energetic asphyxia.

Purpose

Protecting and healing of your aura; balancing the polarities in your psyche.

Description of the Prayer Beads

The string of prayer beads is composed of a total of fifty-nine beads, separated in five series of ten, with a separating bead between each series. A final string separated from the circle has four beads.

Symbolism, Numbers, and General Process

Leukothêa (Μευκοθέα), the White Goddess, will be visualized and invoked during the first cycle of fifty beads. It will be the same for Mêlanotheos (Μελανοθεός), the Dark God, during the second cycle of fifty beads, and Agathodaïmôn (Ἀγαθοδαίμων), the Good Genius, during the last cycle of fifty beads.

Meditation

(The tools for the meditation are optional. You can find their description in the individual ritual that follows this meditation. As usual it is always better, if you can, to use at least a candle.)

Sit comfortably facing east, take your prayer beads, and breathe peacefully for a few minutes.

Use successively the four beads that are separate and on the string outside the circle.

On the first bead, say:

At my left, in the North, I invoke the Earth: Hai Gai!

On the second bead, say:

At my right, in the South, I invoke the Fire: To Pur!

On the third bead, say:

In front of me, in the East, I invoke the Air: Ho Aair!

On the fourth bead, say:

Behind me, in the West, I invoke the Water: To Hudôr!

You will continue with three full cycles of the prayer beads (the five series of ten beads). Each one is associated with one of the three divine names mentioned in the previous paragraph.

First full prayer beads:

• Invocation on the series of beads (fifty invocations): **Hai Leukothêa.**

• Invocation on the separating beads: **Let there be healing!**

Second full prayer beads:

• Invocation on the series of beads (fifty invocations): **Ho Mêlanotheos.**

• Invocation on the separating beads: **Let there be renewal!**

Third full prayer beads:

• Invocation on the series of beads (fifty invocations): **Ho Agathodaïmôn.**

• Invocation on the separating beads: **Let there be blessing!**

When the three full cycles are achieved, keeping your prayer beads in your hand, do the sign of the rose-cross on yourself as follows:

1. Touch your left shoulder, then your right shoulder. During this movement pronounce: **Hai Leukothêa.**

2. Touch your forehead, then your lower abdomen. During this movement pronounce: **Ho Mêlanotheos.**

3. Touch the center of your chest. Maintain this contact while saying: **Ho Agathodaïmôn.**

Release your position.

Stay silent and receptive for a while, then stand up, put the prayer beads aside, and extinguish the candles, saying:

May this light continue to shine in the depths of my being!

Individual Ritual
Tools

Print or draw the symbol of the equal-armed cross. Put it on your altar in front of you. The figure will be oriented east and you will stand to the west, facing east. Place four candles at the top of each part of the cross.[21]

Opening

Take your prayer beads in your left hand and put your thumb and forefinger on the first bead of the independent string that has only four beads. Then with your right hand, light the candle in the north (on your left), which corresponds to the Earth. At the same time, declaim: **Hai Gai.**

Light the candle in the south (on your right), which corresponds to the Fire. At the same time, declaim: **To Pur.**

---

21. You can see a picture of this on my website: www.debiasi.org.

Light the candle in the east, which corresponds to the Air. At the same time, declaim: **Ho Aair.**

Light the candle in the west, which corresponds to the Water. At the same time, declaim: **To Hudôr.**

Cross your arms, left over right, and declaim: **Eimi ho païs tais gais kaï too astêrioo.**[22]

Dedication

Staying in the same position, declaim:

Where there has been sundering let there be healing!

Where there has been searing let there be renewal!

Where there has been banishing let there be blessing!

Let the sacred potency of the Circled Cross, the blazon of Life, Light, and Power, enfold me as a vestment of radiance!

First cycle: Leukothêa

Relax your arms. You can choose the position you consider best for yourself such as sitting on a chair or a cushion, kneeling, or even standing up. You have to be comfortable and able to visualize easily.

Put your fingers on the first separating bead. Then build in front of you the representation of Leukothêa as described in the Ordo Aurum Solis:

---

22. Translation: "And all these things exist in Eternity."

The Great Goddess is robed in a shimmering white peplos,[23] the upper back portion of which is draped to form a covering for her hair. Over this veil she wears a circle of silver, bearing a single beryl cabochon. Her face is almond-shaped with a high forehead and cheekbones. Her customary expression is one of great dignity and gentleness. Her right hand grasps the shaft of the most sacred Double Axe in a specific manner, near the blades, which thus are not raised above the level of her shoulders. The blades of the axe are of silver, the shaft of dark wood; the extremity of the shaft is bound with a bright scarlet thong. Upon her right wrist is a bracelet of special form — each edge has a border of heavy gold, the area between the borders being filled with slender transverse bars of various stones: red, dark green, black, white, yellow, and deep blue. Her left arm is raised, and a seagull with outspread wings is poised upon the palm.

Then say:

Where there has been sundering let there be healing!

Take the first bead of the first decade as you did for the previous beads. On each bead, declaim the name of the divine figure: **Hai Leukothêa!**

Try to keep her presence in mind as you visualize her. If you cannot keep the full visualization, just try to feel her close to you.

On each separating bead, repeat the same declamation you did before on the first bead of the circle. After you have

23. Ancient Greek women wore a body-length robe called "peplos." Various representations can be found on my website: www.debiasi.org.

achieved the five decades, put your fingers on the first separating bead.

Second cycle: Mêlanotheos

Still in this position, build in front of you the representation
of Mêlanotheos as described in the Ordo Aurum Solis:

> The dark God is a male human figure, of muscular
> but slender form, youthful and powerful, dancing and
> wildly ecstatic. His skin is pale indigo. His hair is long
> and dark, and entwined in it are flowers of many col-
> ors. The figure is nude but for a long silver pallium [24]
> draped from his left upper arm. This garment moves
> with the movement of the God, sometimes falling
> across his body, sometimes flowing behind him, some-
> times twining loosely about him. Upon his hair rests
> a crescent of silver light, appearing either as horns of
> power or as the moon.

Then say:

Where there has been searing let there be renewal!

Take the first bead of the first decade as you did for the previous beads. On each bead, declaim the name of the divine
figure: **Ho Mêlanotheos!**

As before, try to keep his presence in mind as you visualize
him.

---

24. A "pallium" is a Roman word for a large cloak that was worn in ancient
Rome and Greece (known in this country as "himation").

When you have achieved the five decades, put your fingers on the first separating bead.

3rd cycle: Agathodaïmôn

Still in this position, build in front of you the representation of Agathodaïmôn as described in the Ordo Aurum Solis:

> The God is a completely human figure, tall and commanding. He has a youthful and spiritual face with a lofty resolute expression and compassionate eyes. His hair is yellow blond and of medium length, falling in curling locks. Upon his head is the golden crown of twelve rays. He wears a white robe, ample and wide-sleeved, which sparkles with light of every color. He also wears a long and wide stole of rich green, embroidered with interlacing of gold. This rests upon his shoulders somewhat away from his neck, the ends falling before him. His feet are bare.

Then say:

Where there has been banishing let there be blessing!

Take the first bead of the first decade as you did for the previous beads. On each bead, declaim the name of the divine figure: **Ho Agathodaïmôn!**

As before, try to keep his presence in mind as you visualize him.

When you have achieved the five decades, put your fingers on the first separating bead.

Affirmation

Continue to hold your prayer beads in your left hand and stand up, facing east. Bring your arms in front of you, widely opened, palms up. Declaim:

Let the sacred potency of the Circled Cross, the blazon of Life, Light, and Power, enfold me as a vestment of radiance!

With the forefinger of your right hand, trace the circled cross in front of you toward the east, as follows.

1. Trace the horizontal line from the left to the right. While tracing this line, vibrate: **Hai Leukothêa!**
2. Trace the vertical line from the top to the bottom. While tracing this line, vibrate: **Ho Mêlanotheos!**
3. Trace the circle clockwise from the top. While tracing this line, vibrate: **Ho Agathodaïmôn!**

When this is done, turn right to face south and proceed in the same way.

Then do the same toward the west and north. Then face east again.

Put your prayer beads in the center of the representation of the circled cross in the center of the four candles.

Raise your arms horizontally on the sides at the level of your shoulders to form a cross with your body. Visualize a golden light going through your arms in a horizontal line. Stay silent for a while and declaim: **êgô leukothêa eimi!** [25]

Visualize the vertical line of golden light going through your spinal column. Stay silent for a while and declaim: **êgô mêlanotheos eimi!**

Put your left hand at the center of your chest and your right hand on the left. Visualize a bright light coming from this center and surrounding you. Stay silent for a while and declaim: **êgô agathodaïmôn eimi!**

Take the pentagram position with your body and declaim:

May the sacred potency of the Circled Cross, the blazon of Life, Light, and Power, enfold me as a vestment of radiance!

Stay silent for a while and release your position.

Closing

Stay silent and receptive for a while, then stand up, put the prayer beads aside, and extinguish the candles, saying:

May this light continue to shine in the depths of my being!

Two-person Ritual
Organization of the Place

The altar will be organized in the same way as you did for the individual ritual.

---

25. Translation: "I am Leukothêa."

One of the two participants will be the receiver of the ritual work. It is best for him to sit on a chair facing east and stay silent during the rituals.

The one doing the ritual will act in the way I described in the introduction of this ritual in order to protect him and activate four powerful seals in his aura. They will be able to welcome good energies and to reject bad influences

Process

Opening

Go in front of the altar. The receiver will be seated behind you.

Proceed as you did in the individual ritual, invoking the four directions as you light the candles:

North—Earth—**Hai Gai**

South—Fire—**To Pur**

East—Air—**Ho Aair**

West—Water—**To Hudôr**

Cross your arms, left over right, declaim: **Eimi ho païs tais gais kaï too astêrioo.**

Dedication

Turn right to face the receiver. Put your prayer beads in contact with the top of his head, your right hand above the left, palm down.

Staying in the same position, declaim:

Where there has been sundering let there be healing!

Where there has been searing let there be renewal!

Where there has been banishing let there be blessing!

Let the sacred potency of the Circled Cross, the blazon of Life, Light, and Power, enfold ... *say the name of the receiver ...* **as a vestment of radiance!**

First cycle: Leukothêa

Go to the north of the receiver, facing him.

Put your fingers on the first separating bead. Then build inwardly the representation of Leukothêa as described previously.

Then say:

Where there has been sundering let there be healing!

Turn the palm of your right hand toward the receiver and take the first bead of the first decade as you did for the previous beads. On each bead, declaim the name of the divine figure:

Hai Leukothêa!

Try to keep your visualization in mind. If you cannot, just focus on the rhythmic pronunciation of the name.

On each separating bead, repeat the same declamation you did before on the first bead of the circle.

When you have achieved the five decades, go to the south of the receiver, facing him.

Second cycle: Mêlanotheos

Put your fingers on the first separating bead. Then build inwardly the representation of Mêlanotheos as described previously.

Then say:

Where there has been searing let there be renewal!

Turn the palm of your right hand toward the receiver and take the first bead of the first decade as you did for the previous beads. On each bead, declaim the name of the divine figure:

Ho Mêlanotheos!

Proceed as you did during the first cycle.

When you have achieved the five decades, go to the east of the receiver, facing him.

Third cycle: Agathodaïmôn

Put your fingers on the first separating bead. Then build inwardly the representation of Agathodaïmôn as described previously.

Then say:

Where there has been banishing let there be blessing!

Turn the palm of your right hand toward the receiver and take the first bead of the first decade as you did for the previous beads. On each bead, declaim the name of the divine figure:

Ho Agathodaïmôn!

Proceed as you did during the first cycle.

Affirmation

Turn the palms of your hands toward the receiver and say:

> **May the sacred potency of the Circled Cross, the blazon of Life, Light, and Power, enfold ... *say the name of the receiver ...* as a vestment of radiance!**

Stay silent for a while, then trace the circled cross in front of the receiver as you did in the individual ritual:

1. Horizontal line (left to right): **Hai Leukothêa!**
2. Vertical line (top to bottom): **Ho Mêlanotheos!**
3. Circle clockwise (from the top): **Ho Agathodaïmôn!**

Move to the south of the receiver and do the same. Continue in the west, north, and return to the east.

Closing

Face east and put your prayer beads on the altar. Turn right, put the palms of your hands upon the head of the receiver, and say:

> **The powerful signs are now sealed in your body of light! May you stay under the protection of the circled cross of light. So mote it be!**

Face east and extinguish the candle, saying:

May this light continue to shine in the depths of our being!

Group Ritual
Organization of the Place

The altar will be organized in the same way as you did for the individual ritual.

One of the participants will be the receiver of the ritual work. It is best for him to sit on a chair facing east and stay silent during the rituals.

Three attendees will be chosen to take the roles of Leukothêa, Mêlanotheos, and Agathodaïmôn.

The other attendees will sit in a circle around the four who will perform directly on the receiver.

Agathodaïmôn will be at the east of the receiver, Leukothêa at the north, and Mêlanotheos at the south.

Process

Opening

The ritual officer who assumes the divine presence of Agathodaïmôn faces east. He invokes the four directions as he lights the candles:

North—Earth—**Hai Gai**

South—Fire—**To Pur**

East—Air—**Ho Aair**

West—Water—**To Hudôr**

He crosses his arms, left over right, and declaims: **Eimi ho països tais gais kaï too astêrioo.**

Dedication

He turns right to face the receiver.

The three ritual officers extend their right arms toward the receiver, palms open.

The ritual officer, facing the candidate, declaims:

Where there has been sundering let there be healing!

Where there has been searing let there be renewal!

Where there has been banishing let there be blessing!

Let the sacred potency of the Circled Cross, the blazon of Life, Light, and Power, enfold ... *say the name of the receiver ...* **as a vestment of radiance!**

The three ritual officers release their right hands.

First cycle: Leukothêa

The ritual officer in the north builds inwardly the representation of Leukothêa as described previously. Everyone in the room visualizes on him the same divine figure. After a few minutes of visualization, the ritual officer who incarnates Leukothêa declaims:

Where there has been sundering let there be healing!

The three ritual officers direct the palms of their right hands toward the receiver. Everyone in the room takes the first bead of the first decade. On each bead, everyone will declaim the name of the divine figure, keeping in mind the visualization:

Hai Leukothêa!

On each separating bead, the ritual officer alone repeats the same declamation as he did before on the first bead of the circle.

When the five decades have been achieved, the three ritual officers release their arms.

Second cycle: Mêlanotheos
The ritual officer in the south builds inwardly the representation of Mêlanotheos as described previously. Everyone in the room visualizes on him the same divine figure. After a few minutes of visualization, the ritual officer who incarnates Mêlanotheos declaims:

Where there has been searing let there be renewal!

The three ritual officers and the attendees proceed as for the first cycle using the visualization and vibration of Mêlanotheos.

Third cycle: Agathodaïmôn
The ritual officer in the east builds inwardly the representation of Agathodaïmôn as described previously. Everyone in the room visualizes on him the same divine figure. After a few

minutes of visualization, the ritual officer who incarnates Agathodaïmôn declaims:

Where there has been banishing let there be blessing!

The three ritual officers and the attendees proceed as for the first cycle using the visualization and vibration of Agathodaïmôn.

Affirmation

One of the attendees stands up and goes to the west of the receiver, facing him.

The four ritual officers turn the palms of their hands toward the receiver and say all together:

May the sacred potency of the Circled Cross, the blazon of Life, Light, and Power, enfold ... *say the name of the receiver ...* **as a vestment of radiance!**

All stay silent for a while, then at the same time, they trace the circled cross toward the receiver, vibrating the three sacred names:

1. Horizontal line (left to right): **Hai Leukothêa!**

2. Vertical line (top to bottom): **Ho Mêlanotheos!**

3. Circle clockwise (from the top): **Ho Agathodaïmôn!**

All release their arms.

Closing

The ritual officer who assumes the divine presence of Agatho-daïmôn faces east and extinguishes the candles, saying:

May this light continue to shine in the depths of our being!

Ritual of the Seven Spheres

Anyone interested in spiritual and esoteric tradition knows that we are surrounded by a body of light often called an "aura." This invisible body is also associated with different waves and flows of energy circulating inside us and all around us. We can compare this circulation to the blood system of our physical body. We can also find specific vortices of energies along the spinal column. They are called "chakras" in the East and "spheres" in the Western tradition. Their number may sometimes be different, but most often, seven main centers are identified. Since its inception, the Hermetic tradition, followed by astrology, associated these energetic vortices to the seven planets. From the bottom to the top you can find: Moon, Mercury, Venus, Sun, Mars, Jupiter, and Saturn. The Ordo Aurum Solis always stayed true to its Hermetic heritage. Several practices use this energetic level according to the traditional teachings going back to Egypt. As the Western Pagan tradition was partly destroyed around the sixth century, several words were lost. This is why we have to dig carefully to find how our ancestors explained these practices. It is not surprising to find precise clues of this use in ancient Egypt and more precisely during the Ptolemaic period (305–30 BCE). The first time I went to Egypt, I spent more than one month visiting the temples and taking the time to enjoy these places, spending hours in the company of the temple guardians. At that time, fundamentalists were not a threat to this country.

One day I stopped in the temple of Denderah, dedicated to the goddesses Hathor and Isis. This temple is famous for the zodiac engraved on the ceiling of one of its chapels. This is a beautiful Ptolemaic temple and the zodiac was built during the first century. Close to these beautiful representations of the seven planets were other chapels depicting the death and resurrection of Osiris. You have to lie on the floor of the temple in order to properly view the engravings inside a kind of well allowing a beam of light to enter the room. The vision of Osiris lying on a bed and surrounded by priests using songs and magnetism to awaken him from death was stunning.

I had to wait several years to deeply experience the connection between the planets of the zodiac and the work of the priests on Osiris. I had to learn specific practices following an Aurum Solis initiation to begin this specific activation of the energetic centers as the Masters of the Golden Chain did at this time. As Demetrius wrote in one of his books (*De Elocutione*), "In Egypt the priests, when singing hymns in praise of the gods employ the seven vowels, which they utter in due succession; and the sound of these letters is so euphonious that men listen to it in place of aulos and cithara."

This knowledge was protected, and the practice you will discover here is one of the manifestations of it.

Purpose

Some of the benefits you will receive from this ritual are to raise your level of consciousness, improve your intuition, connect with the divinities, increase your understanding of astrology, and activate your circulation of subtle energy.

Description of the Prayer Beads

The prayer beads used in this ritual are a circle of forty-nine beads separated in seven series of seven. Between each series there are separating metallic cubes on which the vowels of the Greek alphabet are engraved. The colors of the beads can be different to match the Hermetic colors of the planets, or similar. In this case they will be close to the color of lapis lazuli.

Symbolism, Numbers, and General Process

Here are the main correspondences you have to use.

In the following series, the first indication is the name of the planet, the second is the color, the third is the vowel and the Greek letter, the fourth indication is a part of the body, and the last one is the divinity.

Moon	Silver	**A** (A-Alpha)	Coccyx	Selene
Mercury	Light blue	**E** (E-Epsilon)	Sex organs	Hermes
Venus	Yellow	**H** (H-Eta)	Navel	Aphrodite
Sun	Gold	**I** (I-Iota)	Heart	Helios
Mars	Red	**O** (O-Omicron)	Throat	Ares
Jupiter	White	**U** (Y-Upsilon)	Forehead	Zeus
Saturn	Dark grey	**O** (Ω-Omega)	Top of the head	Cronos

Even if the most important components of this ritual are the vibrations of the letters in a precise sequence, visualizations can be helpful. I recommend using the Greek divinities here as indicated in the chart above. You can find the traditional representations in my book *The Divine Arcana of the Aurum Solis*, and on the Tarot deck of the Aurum Solis.

Three ways can be used in the ritual process: 1. Descent and ascent of the centers; 2. Ascent of the centers; 3. Descent of the centers. It is good to experiment using each one. Here, the first one will be explained.

Meditation

This meditation is a simplified version of the individual ritual. As such, it can concentrate the power of the seven planets and speed the process of attunement with these spheres. You will find it beneficial to use this meditation process at any time during the day when it is not possible to perform the full individual ritual.

Feel free to use the tools described in the following part (individual ritual) of this chapter.

Light the candles.

Sit comfortably facing east. Take your prayer beads, and breathe peacefully for a few minutes.

You can choose between two possibilities, ascent or descent, by using the planetary spheres.

In any of these movements, you pronounce the vowel of the planet once per bead in the series.

The ascendant sequence is: **Alpha** (Moon), **Epsilon** (Mercury), **Eta** (Venus), **Iota** (Sun), **Omicron** (Mars), **Upsilon** (Jupiter), **Omega** (Saturn).

The descending sequence is the reverse: **Omega, Upsilon, Omicron, Iota, Eta, Epsilon, Alpha**.

Only the vowels are pronounced and not their full name. I already explained their pronunciation in Chapter 3 of this book, "Blessing of Your Prayer Beads."

You can also link both sequences by doing the first one followed by the second one.

When your planned sequence has been performed, stay silent and receptive for a while. Then stand up, put the prayer beads aside, and extinguish the candles, saying:

May this light continue to shine in the depths of my being!

Individual Ritual
Tools

A representation of the Hermetic Macrocosm[26] can be used for this ritual. It should be hung on the wall in front of you.

You will place seven colored lamps (or seven plain beeswax candles) on your altar.[27] It is good to put the seven cards of the Aurum Solis Tarot on the outer side of each light.

At the beginning, your prayer beads will be at the center of the seven-pointed star.

Opening

In order to invoke the divine powers and welcome them into your inner being, into your aura, stand up in front of your altar and visualize the symbol of the Glorious Star above your

---

26. This representation can be found on my website: www.debiasi.org.
27. A diagram for this can be found on my website: www.debiasi.org.

head. Hold this glorious symbol in your mind, raise your arms up to the sky, palms up, and declaim one time:

En Giro Torte Sol Ciclos Et Rotor Igne.

Lower your arms, allowing them to hang naturally at your sides.

First cycle—Descent

1. Take your prayer beads in your left hand and put your thumb and forefinger on the first bead engraved with the Greek letter **O** (Omega).

With your right hand, light the first flame (Saturn). Then close (or half close) your eyes and visualize a golden light coming from the center of the star and descending in a sphere just above the top of your head.

Keeping in mind this center of energy, move your fingers on the first bead of the series and vibrate the vowel of the sphere. Continue seven times.

2. Put your thumb and forefinger on the bead engraved with the Greek letter **U** (Upsilon).

With your right hand, light the second flame (Jupiter). Then close (or half close) your eyes and visualize a golden light descending through the center of the spinal column from this upper sphere to a second sphere, which is situated at the level of the forehead.

Keeping in mind this center of energy, move your fingers on the first bead of the series and vibrate the vowel of the sphere. Continue seven times.

3. Put your thumb and forefinger on the bead engraved with the Greek letter **O** (Omicron).

With your right hand, light the third flame (Mars). Then proceed as you did previously, now visualizing a golden light descending to the sphere situated at the level of the throat.

Vibrate the vowel of the sphere on the seven beads of this series.

4. Put your thumb and forefinger on the bead engraved with the Greek letter **I** (Iota).

With your right hand, light the fourth flame (Sun). Then proceed as you did previously, now visualizing a golden light descending to the sphere situated at the level of the heart.

Vibrate the vowel of the sphere on the seven beads of this series.

5. Put your thumb and forefinger on the bead engraved with the Greek letter **H** (Eta).

With your right hand, light the fifth flame (Venus). Then proceed as you did previously, now visualizing a golden light descending to the sphere situated at the level of the navel.

Vibrate the vowel of the sphere on the seven beads of this series.

6. Put your thumb and forefinger on the bead engraved with the Greek letter **E** (Epsilon).

With your right hand, light the sixth flame (Mercury). Then proceed as you did previously, now visualizing a golden light descending to the sphere situated at the level of the sex organs (more precisely, three inches above the sex organs).

Vibrate the vowel of the sphere on the seven beads of this series.

7. Put your thumb and forefinger on the bead engraved with the Greek letter **A** (Alpha).

With your right hand, light the seventh flame (Moon). Then proceed as you did previously, now visualizing a golden light descending to the sphere situated at the level of the coccyx.

Vibrate the vowel of the sphere on the seven beads of this series.

8. Now follow your natural breath.

Hold in your consciousness and strengthen all the centers that you just activated, and the vertical column of light that connects them.

For a few moments, be aware of the ground on which you stand, and the sensation of your feet on the floor.

You can sit now if you want.

Second cycle—Ascent

1. Put your thumb and forefinger on the bead engraved with the Greek letter **A** (Alpha).

Focus your consciousness on the center located at the level of your coccyx. Intensify its brightness and vibrate the vowel of the sphere on the seven beads of this series.

2. Put your thumb and forefinger on the bead engraved with the Greek letter **E** (Epsilon).

While keeping in mind your previous visualizations, visualize two streams of white light emanating simultaneously left and right from the center of your lower spine and rising to enter the upper center located at the sex organs.

Focus your consciousness on this sphere. Intensify its brightness and vibrate the vowel of the sphere on the seven beads of this series.

3. Put your thumb and forefinger on the bead engraved with the Greek letter **H** (Eta).

Visualize in the same way the light strips extending from each side of the previous sphere to the next sphere located at the navel.

Intensify the brightness of the center and vibrate the vowel of the sphere on the seven beads of this series.

Do the same for the following centers:

4. Heart: **I** (I-Iota).

5. Throat: **O** (O-Omicron).

6. Forehead: **U** (U-Upsilon).

7. Top of the head: **O** (Ω-Omega).

Increase the light in this center of power and visualize the light ascending above your head.

Visualize a veil and then put your consciousness at the same level as the veil.

Now, visualize the Glorious Star higher above your head. Then say the following invocation eight times:

En Giro Torte Sol Ciclos Et Rotor Igne.

Visualize your aura of intense, bright, golden light that shines all around you and within you.

Then return to the awareness of your body.

Closing

Stay silent and receptive for a while, then stand up, put the prayer beads aside, extinguish the candles in the reverse sequence of the lighting, and say:

May this spiritual light continue to enlighten my body of light!

Two-person Ritual
Organization of the Place

As for the individual ritual, a representation of the Hermetic Macrocosm can be hung on the wall in front of you.

At the center of the room, you will install a double circle large enough to allow the couple to be in the center. These circles can be drawn on the floor or created with cords. In the ring you will place seven colored lamps (or seven plain beeswax candles) according to the diagram provided on my website. It is good to put the seven cards of the Aurum Solis Tarot beside each light.

Depending on the choice of the receiver, you will put a cushion or a chair at the center of the circle. He must sit on it, keeping his back straight.

Both participants will have their prayer beads in hand.

Process

Opening

The receiver at the center of the circle visualizes the symbol of the Glorious Star above his head. Meanwhile, the second one goes behind the receiver and extends his arms toward the top of his head. He also visualizes this glorious symbol. Then both of them declaim:

En Giro Torte Sol Ciclos Et Rotor Igne.

The receiver closes his eyes and the second one goes in front of the light associated with Saturn to light it.

First cycle—Descent

1. Both have their prayer beads in their hands (right for the receiver, left for the other).

The Magus of the ritual lights the candle and at the same time vibrates in the Greek letter **O** (Omega).

Then the receiver visualizes a golden light coming from the center of the star and descending in a sphere just above the top of his head. At the same time, the Magus visualizes this light coming from the top into the circle.

Keeping in mind this visualization, both move their fingers successively on the seven beads of this series. On each, they vibrate the vowel of the sphere.

2. The Magus goes in front of the light associated with Jupiter in order to light it.

The Magus lights the candle and at the same time vibrates in the Greek letter **U** (Upsilon).

Then the receiver visualizes a golden light descending through the center of the spinal column from this upper sphere to a second sphere, which is situated at the level of the forehead. At the same time, the Magus visualizes this light coming from the top into the circle.

Keeping this visualization in mind, both move their fingers successively on the seven beads of this series. On each, they vibrate the vowel of the sphere.

They do the same for the following spheres:

3. Mars—Throat—**O** (Omicron)

4. Sun—Heart—**I** (Iota)

5. Venus—Navel—**H** (Eta)

6. Mercury—Sex Organs—**E** (Epsilon)

7. Moon—Coccyx—**A** (Alpha)

8. Both hold in their consciousness all the spheres they just activated, and the vertical column of light that connects them.

Second cycle—Ascent

1. The Magus comes behind the receiver. He extends his right arm to put his right hand upon the head of the receiver.

His thumb and forefinger of his left hand are on the bead engraved with the Greek letter **A** (A-Alpha). He vibrates this vowel once.

Then together, they focus their consciousness on the center of the receiver located at the level of his coccyx. Both intensify the brightness and vibrate the vowel of the sphere on the seven beads of this series.

2. Keeping the same position, the Magus puts his thumb and forefinger on the bead engraved with the Greek letter **E** (E-Epsilon).

As previously, he vibrates the vowel once. While keeping in mind their previous visualizations, both visualize the two streams of white light emanating simultaneously left and right from the center of the lower spine of the receiver, and rising to enter the upper center located at the sex organs.

Focusing their consciousness on this sphere, both intensify the brightness and vibrate the vowel of the sphere on the seven beads of this series.

They do the same for the following centers:

3. Navel: **H** (Eta).

4. Heart: **I** (Iota).

5. Throat: **O** (Omicron).

6. Forehead: **U** (Upsilon).

7. Top of the head: **O** (Omega).

8. Both visualize the light ascending above the head of the receiver to the Glorious Star. Then they say together the following invocation eight times:

En Giro Torte Sol Ciclos Et Rotor Igne.

The aura shines all around them and fills out the whole circle.

The Magus releases his hand and they return to the awareness of their bodies.

Closing

Stay silent and receptive for a while. Then the Magus puts his prayer beads aside, and extinguishes the candles in the reverse sequence of the lighting.

He goes in front of the receiver, puts his hand on the top of his head and says:

May this spiritual light continue to enlighten your body of light!

So mote it be!

GROUP RITUAL
Organization of the Place

As before in this ritual, hang a representation of the Hermetic Macrocosm on the east wall.

The chairs are organized in a circle, facing the center.

An altar will be placed at the center of the circle. Its height will be the approximate level of the chairs. On top of the altar, the tools will be organized in the same way as in the individual ritual.

Process

Opening

The Magus for the ceremony will stand and light the lamps in the usual sequence: Saturn, Jupiter, Mars, Sun, Venus, Mercury, and Moon.

Then he sits, and everyone puts his left hand on the right forearm (or thigh) of the person on his left.

Everyone visualizes the Glorious Star on the top of his head. Then all declaim:

En Giro Torte Sol Ciclos Et Rotor Igne.

First cycle—Descent

The process of the descent is performed as for the individual ritual. All vibrate the vowels at the same time. The first time you perform this ritual in a group it is a good idea to choose someone who will lead the group in order to obtain a powerful and regular rhythm of the vibrations.

When the descent is achieved, everyone releases his left hand.

Second cycle—Ascent

The process of the ascent is performed as for the individual ritual and all the vibrations are performed simultaneously.

When the seven spheres have been visualized and the vowels vibrated, all stand and visualize the light ascending above their heads to the Glorious Star. Then all declaim:

En Giro Torte Sol Ciclos Et Rotor Igne.

Closing

The Magus extinguishes the candles in the reverse sequence the beginning.

All declaim:

May this spiritual light continue to enlighten my body of light!

So mote it be!

You can sit to meditate for a few minutes.

Ritual of the Spiritual Ladder

The "spiritual ladder" is a Hermetic representation of the cosmos, which has been hidden for centuries in the most obvious ritual principles used in the modern Western tradition. When I performed my first rituals from the Wiccan tradition, I was happy to use this ancient connection between the four elements and the four directions. As previously noted, Qabalah is an interesting system, but from my initiation in the Aurum Solis I was always disturbed by the frequent disconnection with authentic Hermetism. One of the most obvious aspects was what I like to call the "missing first element": Earth. Of course, "mother letters" are fundamental in the Hebrew language, but there are only three of them: Aleph (Air), Mem (Water), and Shin (Fire). When you are eager to use Qabalah in a magick or Theurgic way, such a situation is disturbing. I will talk later about Druidism and Wicca, but even for Hermetism, Qabalah is much too limited to a specific theological representation of the world.

From its beginning, Western tradition used four elements (plus one: Aether) and these are the first four steps of this ascension.

Astrology is the key of following two levels. It is clear that you can learn astrology, understand its symbolism, and never perform any magical rituals. However, the contrary is quite impossible. The planets and the zodiac are powers with which you must create a strong and conscious link. There are several ways to do that.

The one you will use in these rituals comes from a Hermetic ritual developed in the Kabbalistic Order of the Rose-Cross. Using this specific prayer beads ritual was not the original idea of the ritual's creator, but was developed to allow the initiates to integrate this spiritual process. In order to reach the deepest part of your psyche, it is useful to associate mantras (rhythmic pronunciations), movements, and visualizations. This is what you will do here.

Description of the Prayer Beads

This prayer beads string is made of forty-eight beads. Twelve are on a separate string and the thirty-six others are organized in a circle. These thirty-six beads are separated into twelve groups of three. They are deep blue. The twelve others are separated in two groups, of five and seven. The colors of the first group are: dark grey, deep blue, light blue, red, and white. The colors of the second group are: silver, light blue, yellow, gold, red, white, and dark gray.

Symbolism, Numbers, and General Process

You will find diagrams on my website (www.debiasi.org) that show the connections between the elements, the planets, and the signs of the zodiac. Another diagram shows the travels you must do during the ritual. There are situations in which you cannot move: too little room, people around you, etc. In these situations you will have to simply close your eyes and visualize the moves as if you were doing them.

Don't forget that you can perform this ritual outdoors. It is also good to realize that your feelings will be different at night and during the day. I suggest you try both.

As you can easily understand, your ritual practice will allow you to ascend the Hermetic cosmos. This ascent associates two levels, which correspond to the macrocosm and microcosm. This is one example of rising to the planes.

Meditation

Feel free to use the tools described in the following section (individual ritual) of this chapter.

Light the candles.

Sit comfortably facing east. Breathe peacefully for a few minutes.

Take your prayer beads in your hand, using first the separate string on which you can see the twelve beads.

On the first one, say:

O powers of the Earth, I invoke you!

On the second one, say:

O powers of the Waters, I invoke you!

On the third one, say:

O powers of the Fires, I invoke you!

On the fourth one, say:

O powers of the Skies, I invoke you!

On the fifth one, say:

O power of the Aether, I invoke you!

Continue on the seven following beads, using the seven Greek vowels as in the previous part of this chapter, "Ritual of the Seven Spheres":

Alpha (Moon), **Epsilon** (Mercury), **Eta** (Venus), **Iota** (Sun), **Omicron** (Mars), **Upsilon** (Jupiter), **Omega** (Saturn).

Continue this meditation using the circle of beads. Pronounce the name of the divinity three times on each bead. By doing this, the same name will be declaimed nine times by each group of three beads.

1. Athena; 2. Aphrodite; 3. Apollo; 4. Hermes; 5. Zeus; 6. Demeter; 7. Hephaestos; 8. Ares; 9. Artemis; 10. Hestia; 11. Hera; 12. Poseidon.

When the full prayer beads ritual has been performed, stay silent and receptive for a while. Then stand up, put the prayer beads aside, and extinguish the candles, saying:

May this light continue to shine in the depths of my being!

Individual Ritual
Tools

Just as for the Ritual of the Seven Spheres, the representation of the Hermetic Macrocosm can be used for this ritual. It is good to hang it on the east wall.

You will put your altar in the center of the room. It will be covered with a white altar cloth. Put the tools that are indicated below on the top of it. If you have the Aurum Solis Tarot Deck, feel free to use it in the ritual. If not, just write down the names (and visualizations) needed for this ritual on white index cards.

- Lamp (or plain beeswax candle)
- Censer (with incense)
- Prayer beads

Opening
The foundation

Stand to the west of the altar, facing east. Breathe in silence for a while, aware of your body and the place.

Light the candle. Light the incense and raise the censer toward the sky, saying:

Hear me, O Gods, you who hold the rudder of sacred wisdom. Lead us mortals back among the immortals as you light in our souls the flame of return. May the

ineffable initiations of your hymns give us the power
to escape the dark cave of our lives and purify ourselves.

Hearken, powerful liberators!

Dispel the surrounding obscurity, and grant me the
power to understand the holy books; replace the darkness with a pure and holy light. Thus may I truly know
the incorruptible God that I am.

May a wicked spirit never keep me overwhelmed by
ills, submerged in the waters of forgetfulness and far
away from the Gods and Goddesses.

May my soul not be fettered in the jails of life where I
am left to suffer a terrifying atonement in the icy cycles
of generation. I do not want to wander anymore.

O you, sovereign Gods of radiant wisdom, hear me!
Reveal to one who hastens on the Path of Return the
holy ecstasies and the initiations held in the depth of
your sacred words!

Replace the censer on the altar.

Then take the Tarot deck (or the white cards you prepared)
in your left hand. Take your prayer beads in your right hand
and put your thumb and forefinger on the first bead of the
series of five of the independent string that has twelve beads.

Go to the east of the room and declaim: **Ho Aair.**

Go to the south. If you have the cards in hand, put the one you just used under the deck, and now use the second card. (You will proceed in the same way for all the other steps.) With your fingers on the second bead, declaim: **To Pur.**

Go to the west. With your fingers on the third bead, declaim: **To Hudôr.**

Go to the north. With your fingers on the fourth bead, declaim: **Hai Gai.**

Come back to the east, raise your arms toward the sky and declaim: **Hai Aïthair.**

Cross your arms, left over right, and declaim:

Eimi ho païs tais gais kaï too astêrioo.

The Seven Spheres

Go to the west, facing east. Breathe and relax for a few seconds.

First step: Visualize in front of you a drape made of rippling silver light. Taking the first bead of the series of seven on the separated string between your thumb and forefinger, vibrate seven times the vowel of the sphere: **A** (Alpha). Then vibrate one time the name of the divinity of this sphere (Selene) and at the same time, take a step forward toward the altar. Feel the silver light all around you and inside you.

Release the visualization.

Second step: Visualize in front of you a drape made of rippling light-blue light. Taking the second bead of this series, vibrate seven times the vowel of the sphere: **E** (Epsilon). Then vibrate one time the name of the divinity of this sphere (Hermes) and at the same time, take a step forward toward the altar. Feel the light-blue light all around you and inside you.

Release the visualization.

Proceed in the same way for the following five steps according to the instructions below.

Third step: Color: Yellow—Vowel: **H** (Eta)—Divinity: Aphrodite.

Fourth step: Color: Gold—Vowel: **I** (Iota)—Divinity: Helios.

Fifth step: Color: Red—Vowel: **O** (Omicron)—Divinity: Ares.

Sixth step: Color: White—Vowel: **U** (Upsilon)—Divinity: Zeus.

Seventh step: Color: Dark grey—Vowel: **O** (Omega)—Divinity: Cronos.

The Zodiac

You are now in front of your altar. Turn to your right to begin a counterclockwise circumambulation. Move your fingers on the first bead of the first series of three. You will perform the circumambulation in twelve steps, which correspond to the twelve signs of the zodiac. At each step you will visualize the divinity and take a step forward to be beside him (or her). You will pronounce the divine name three times, one on each bead of the series.

In the list below, the first indication is the number of the step and the second is the name of the divinity.

1st step: Athena—2nd step: Aphrodite—3rd step: Apollo—4th step: Hermes—5th step: Zeus—6th step: Demeter—7th step: Hephaestos—8th step: Ares—9th step: Artemis—10th step: Hestia—11th step: Hera—12th step: Poseidon

When you are back at your starting point, turn to face east and put your Tarot (if you used one) and the prayer beads on the altar.

You can sit to meditate for a while. When you feel the moment is right, stand up.

Closing

Raise your hands toward the sky and declaim:

May the divine order of the cosmos harmonize all aspects of my life!

May the powers of the stars lead my life to a successful realization!

May the skies be propitious to me in all aspects of my life!

So mote it be!

Extinguish the candle.

Two-person Ritual
Organization of the Place

The place will be prepared as for the individual ritual.

You will add a chair on the west side of the room and a blindfold for the one who will be the receiver.

Just as for the individual ritual, the representation of the Hermetic Macrocosm is hung on the east wall of the room.

Both of you will have prayer beads in your hands.

Process

Opening

Both of you go to the west of the altar, facing east. Breathe in silence for a while, aware of your body and the place.

One of you lights the candle. The other lights the incense and raises the censer toward the sky. The other one raises his arms. Both of you declaim the hymn to the Gods:

Hear me, O Gods ... *(See individual ritual)*

The censer is replaced on the altar.

The receiver takes his prayer beads, goes to the west and sits on the chair. The Magus puts a blindfold on him.

Standing in front of him (east of the receiver), the Magus visualizes a pure wind blowing on the receiver. With his thumb and forefinger on the first bead of the series of five of the independent string that has twelve beads, he vibrates: **Ho Aair.**

He goes to the south of the receiver, facing him. He visualizes the heat of a purifying fire reaching the receiver. With his fingers on the second bead, he vibrates: **To Pur.**

He proceeds in the same way from the west [**To Hudôr**] and to the north [**Hai Gai**].

He comes back to the east, again facing the receiver, raises his arms and vibrates: **Hai aïthair.**

He crosses his arms, left over right, and declaims:

Eimi ho païs tais gais kaï too astêrioo.

The Seven Spheres

Having the prayer beads in his left hand, the Magus will direct his right palm toward the centers of the receiver. For each center, he will visualize the color and the power in these centers and vibrate seven times (on each bead of the series of seven) the vowel associated with it.

The receiver can vibrate at the same time, but in a lower voice. He will not try to visualize.

For the first two centers of energy, the Magus will go behind the receiver. He will come back to the east of him and face him for the five other centers.   .

1. Moon—Coccyx—**A** (Alpha)

6. Mercury—Sex Organs—**E** (Epsilon)

5. Venus—Navel—**H** (Heta)

4. Sun—Heart—**I** (Iota)

5. Mars—Throat—**O** (Omicron)

3. Jupiter—Forehead—**U** (Upsilon)

7. Saturn—Top of the Head—**O** (Omega)

The Zodiac

The Magus will perform a counterclockwise circumambulation. He will proceed as for the individual ritual, but around the receiver and always keeping the palm of his right hand in his direction. This circumambulation will be performed in twelve steps. He will visualize the divinity in himself as if he is the divinity. The divine name will be vibrated three times, one on each bead of the series.

The receiver chooses to pronounce with the Magus.

When this circle is achieved, the Magus brings back his prayer beads to the altar, goes in front of the receiver, and puts the palms of his hands above his head.

Closing

The Magus declaims:

May the divine order of the cosmos harmonize all aspects of your life!

May the powers of the stars lead your life to a successful realization!

May the skies be propitious to you in all aspects of your life!

So mote it be!

After a moment of silence, he removes the blindfold, turns to the east, and goes to the altar to extinguish the candle.

GROUP RITUAL
Organization of the Place

The place will be prepared as for the two-person ritual.

Process

Opening

The Magus goes to the west of the altar, facing east.

Everyone faces east.

The Magus lights the candle and the incense, and raises the censer toward the sky. All the participants raise their arms and declaim the hymn to the Gods:

Hear me, O Gods ... *(See individual ritual).*

The censer is replaced on the altar.

The receiver goes to the west and sits on the chair. The Magus blindfolds him.

All stand in a circle around him and visualize a pure wind blowing from the east and filling out the circle. All have their thumb and forefinger on the first bead of the series of five of the independent string that has twelve beads. They vibrate: **Ho Aair.**

All visualize the heat of a purifying fire coming from the south and filling out the circle. With their fingers on the second bead, all vibrate: **To Pur.**

They proceed in the same way with the Water from the west [**To Hudôr**] and the Earth from the north [**Hai Gai**].

All visualize a pure golden light coming from above. They vibrate: **Hai Aïthair.**

The Seven Spheres

All will follow the process of the seven spheres, visualizing the light in the seven spheres of the receiver increasing in power. All will vibrate at the same time.

1. Moon—Coccyx—**A** (Alpha)

6. Mercury—Sex Organs—**E** (Epsilon)

5. Venus—Navel—**H** (Heta)

4. Sun—Heart—**I** (Iota)

5. Mars—Throat—**O** (Omicron)

3. Jupiter—Forehead—**U** (Upsilon)

7. Saturn—Top of the Head—**O** (Omega)

The Zodiac

All the participants perform a counterclockwise circumambulation in twelve steps. Their visualization will focus on increasing the golden light in their circle and aura. At each step, all pronounce the name of the divinity of the sign three times, one pronunciation on each bead of the series of three.

When this circle is achieved, all face east.

Closing

The Magus declaims:

May the divine order of the cosmos harmonize all aspects of the life of ... *name of the receiver ...* **!**

May the powers of the stars lead his life to a successful realization!

May the skies be propitious to him in all aspects of his life!

So mote it be!

After a moment of silence, one of the participants removes the receiver's blindfold.

Then the Magus extinguishes the candle.

Ritual of the Hermetic Palindrome

The Italian city of Florence is a sacred place for the Ogdoadic and Hermetic tradition of the Aurum Solis. During the Renaissance, it was there that the golden chain of the adepts was formally reactivated. Several places and monuments of this city received the mark of this inheritance. Clues are everywhere for those who know how to look. The shape of buildings, their pavement, ceiling, etc., are signs that can be obvious or not. In the center of this great city, the cathedral and the baptistery are among the obvious.

In Italy it is usual for worshippers to visit churches with prayer beads in their hands. It was not unusual for me to do the same and walk in the baptistery with the same ritual instrument in my hands. I had already gone to this place a few times, but this was the first time I had planned to do my journey differently. Who would have noticed that my prayer beads were a little different from the Christian ones? After all, beads are beads! In this baptistery, all is built according to the ancient principles of the Hermetic tradition. The numbers twelve and eight are everywhere: on the floor and in the shape of the building. One mosaic at the entrance of the baptistery is a remarkable astrological mosaic. The center is marked by a sun with twelve rays surrounded by a mysterious sentence composed of eight words: "En Giro Torte Sol Ciclos Et Rotor Igne." Around the sun, two other concentric circles are associated with the twelve signs of the zodiac. This mosaic is well-oriented on the axis east-west, the entrance being in the east (facing the entrance of the cathedral). Each word is also associated with the eight directions facing each side of the building. Knowing these elements, it was easy to go to the north of the palindrome and begin this meditative Ogdoadic journey. In an instant I was isolated, far from the visitors busy contemplating the famous mosaics of the ceiling. The use of these Ogdoadic prayer beads is powerful, and even if you are not in the center of this symbolic building, you will be able, as I was, to deeply connect to this source.

Purpose

This ritual is best for introspection, finding the origin of a problem and mental block, increasing your inner energy, harmonization with the Hermetic tradition, and activating your solar center (and solar body).

Description of the Prayer Beads

The prayer beads are composed of eight series of eight turquoise beads with four separating beads. A golden tassel is attached to them.

Symbolism, Numbers, and General Process

I already spoke in the introduction of this ritual about the symbolic connection of these prayer beads with architecture and the Ogdoad. As a basis for this ritual, you must keep in mind that each series of eight beads corresponds to each word of this magical sentence. At the same time, and to allow you to go further, each word is also associated with a direction of the space. I summarize for you these correspondences below.

The list below provides the name to pronounce and the direction of the space.

First series: **En**—North

Second series: **Giro**—Northeast

Third series: **Torte**—East

Fourth series: **Sol**—Southeast

Fifth series: **Ciclos**—South

Sixth series: **Et**—Southwest

Seventh series: **Rotor**—West

Eighth series: **Igne**—Northwest

The uses of these prayer beads are countless. They can be used in various ways in rituals, but also as mantric support during a meditative walk outside. The latter is one of the group practices I organized from time to time in the Mojave Desert around Las Vegas. They are also part of the magical training of the Aurum Solis. Of course, it is better to have tutors to perform this kind of practice. But you can try right now, anywhere in the country. A wild place is often better.

The explanation is simple; the practice requires little training. Take your prayer beads in your hands, and begin to walk, just being aware of your physical sensations. After a few minutes, you can begin to use the prayer beads. You must associate one bead with one word, with one step. Each time you put a foot on the ground, you pronounce one word of the sentence, and progress to the next bead. You have to find the correct rhythm adapted to your walk. At the same time, you must release any thoughts, just feeling your body, your feet, the sound, etc. This meditative practice is powerful and efficient. Its consequences are impressive and will increase your magical potential in a huge way.

Here you will use the prayer beads according to one of the techniques used inside, similar to what I did in Florence.

Meditation

Feel free to use the tools described in the following section (individual ritual) of this chapter.

Light the candles.

Sit comfortably facing east. Breathe peacefully for a few minutes.

Take your prayer beads in your hand. You can perform at least one full prayer beads cycle composed of eight series. You can do more if you want to go deeper in this meditation, but keep in mind that in this case, you must achieve a full cycle of eight series and not stop in the middle.

On each bead of a series, you will pronounce the mystical palindrome:

En giro torte sol ciclos et rotor igne.

On each separating bead, you must declaim:

I am the Sun!

I am the wheel moved by the fire!

I am the center of the power which moves the spheres!

When your cycle has been achieved, stay silent and receptive for a while. Then stand up, put the prayer beads aside, and extinguish the candles, saying:

May this light continue to shine in the depths of my being!

Individual Ritual
Tools

If you can, put the representation of the pavement of the Florence baptistery on the east wall of your room.

You will put your altar in the center of the room. It will be covered with a white altar cloth. On the center, put the representation of the eight-pointed star inside an octagon.[28] Place eight lamps (or plain beeswax candles) at each angle.

Put a censer in the exact center of the representations. As incense you can use "Dragonblood" or a specific one from the Aurum Solis tradition, but avoid any mixed preparations.

Your prayer beads are on the altar.

Opening

Stand to the west of the altar, facing east. Breathe in silence for a while, aware of your body and the place.

Light the candles in the sequence indicated on the representation; each time you light a candle, you will pronounce the palindrome.

When this is done, light the incense and raise the censer, saying:

May the eight divine powers of the Ogdoad be honored and worshipped!

---

28. A representation of this can be found on my website: www.debiasi.org.

May their divine presence be manifested in the eight directions of the place where I stand now!

May their light illuminate the secret octagonal room of my Noûs!

Replace the censer on the center of the altar and take your prayer beads in your right hand.

Go to the north of the altar, facing east, and declaim:

May the Sun be worshipped as he always has been by the initiates of the golden chain!

The Mystical Journey

You will perform eight circumambulations clockwise, taking eight steps around the altar. Each step will be associated with one bead. Thus, one series of eight beads allows you to perform one circumambulation. The full prayer beads will allow you to achieve eight circumambulations.

It is important to find a regular pace, and to be aware of this complex (and simple) combination of movements of your fingers on the beads, your pace, and the pronunciations. On each bead, you pronounce:

En giro torte sol ciclos et rotor igne.

When the circumambulations are complete, come back to the west, facing east.

Put the prayer beads back on the altar. Open your arms wide toward the east and the banner. The palms of your hands are up. Visualize yourself surrounded by a powerful light. Rays of light are shining from you, illuminating your aura and the whole place.

Declaim:

I am the Sun!

I am the wheel moved by the fire!

I am the center of the power which moves the spheres!

Keep the position for a few seconds and release your arms in silence.

Closing

Stay silent and receptive for a while. You can also sit and meditate.

Then stand up and declaim:

The spiritual light has been invoked and activated. As the source of all life, let it stay as the secret power of my life!

Extinguish the candles in the reverse sequence.

Two-person Ritual
Organization of the Place

Organize the place as you did for the individual ritual.

Process

Opening

The two participants stand to the west of the altar, facing east. They breathe in silence for a while, aware of their bodies and the place.

One of them will light the candles in the sequence indicated in the individual ritual. Each time he lights a candle, both of them pronounce one word of the palindrome. The eight lights will allow pronouncing the whole sentence.

When this is done, one goes to the north of the altar, facing south. The other will go to the south of the altar, facing his partner.

The one in the south lights the incense.

Both of them turn their hands toward the smoke of the incense, saying:

May the eight divine powers of the Ogdoad be honored and worshipped!

May their divine presence be manifested in the eight directions of the place where we stand now!

May their light illuminate the secret octagonal room of our Noûs!

Both of them take their prayer beads in their right hand. They turn to face the direction allowing them to perform the clockwise circumambulations.

The Mystical Journey

Both will perform one circumambulation clockwise, composed of eight stops around the altar. These stations will be located in the eight directions of the space associated with each side of the octagon, which is on the altar.

One series of eight beads will be used in each direction. On each bead, the mystical palindrome "**En giro torte sol ciclos et rotor igne**" is declaimed. The full prayer beads will allow you to achieve one full circumambulation around the altar. It is important to remember that the walk must be symmetrical and performed at the same time. The pronunciations have to be synchronic, too. At each time around, the positions of the two partners must be symmetric.

When the circumambulation is complete, both of them must face the altar.

They put their prayer beads back on the altar. They open their arms wide toward the center. The palms of their hands are up. They visualize themselves surrounded by a powerful light. Rays of light are shining from them, illuminating their auras and the whole place.

Both of them declaim simultaneously:

I am the Sun!

I am the wheel moved by the fire!

I am the center of the power which moves the spheres!

They keep the position for a few seconds and release their arms in silence.

Closing

They may remain silent and receptive for a while. They may also sit and meditate.

Then they stand up and declaim:

The spiritual light has been invoked and activated. As the source of all life, let it stay as the secret power of my life!

The one who did not light the candles extinguishes them in the reverse sequence.

GROUP RITUAL
Organization of the Place

Organize the place as you did for the individual ritual. Usually, this group ritual is performed with eight participants. You can organize the practice with fewer, but an even number is better. If possible, it is good to have an extra participant outside the group. He will use a bell or a gong to synchronize the group's progression.

Process

Opening

The participants take their place in the eight directions around the altar, facing the center. They breathe in silence for a while, aware of their bodies and the place.

The participant in the north lights the candles in the sequence indicated in the individual ritual. Each time he lights a candle, everyone pronounces one word of the palindrome.

When this is done, the one in the south lights the incense.

Everyone joins hands to make a chain. As the smoke of the incense is rising, they declaim:

May the eight divine powers of the Ogdoad be honored and worshipped!

May their divine presence be manifested in the eight directions of the place where we stand now!

May their light illuminate the secret octagonal room of our Noûs!

All the participants take their prayer beads in their right hand. They turn to face the direction allowing them to perform the clockwise circumambulations.

The Mystical Journey

Just as for the couple ritual, they will perform circumambulations clockwise, composed of eight stops around the altar. These stations will be located in the eight directions of the space associated with each side of the octagon, which is on the altar.

On this point, the process is the same as for the couple. The full prayer beads will allow you to achieve one full circumambulation around the altar. Again, the walk must be symmetric and performed at the same time. The pronunciations must be synchronic, too. To facilitate this progression, the participant who is outside the circle knocks the gong at the end of each series. At this sound, everyone moves to the next position.

When the circumambulation is complete, the assistant knocks the gong eight consecutive times. The last sound is a bit higher. Then a new circumambulation begins.

The full process will be composed of eight circumambulations performed in the same way.

When the eight circles are achieved, the assistant knocks the gong five times.

Everyone faces the altar and replaces his prayer beads on it.

They open their arms wide toward the center. The palms of their hands are up. They visualize themselves surrounded by a powerful light. Rays of light are shining from them, illuminating their auras and the whole place.

Everyone declaims simultaneously:

I am the Sun!

I am the wheel moved by the fire!

I am the center of the power which moves the spheres!

They keep the position for a few seconds and release their arms in silence.

Closing

They may remain silent and receptive for a while. They may also sit and meditate.

Then they stand up and declaim:

The spiritual light has been invoked and activated. As the source of all life, let it stay as the secret power of my life!

The one in the south extinguishes the candles in the reverse sequence.

Chapter 6

Wiccan Tradition

Wicca is an amazing tradition founded by Gerald Gardner after World War II. Here is not the place to tell the history of Wicca or to analyze the sources used by its founder. The Wiccan rituals use elements and symbols that come from old European traditions. Even if the sources are numerous, this entire cultural and magic heritage helped to build an original and very interesting system. Wicca can be simply defined as a religion rooted in ceremonial magic with strong influences of Mediterranean Pagan traditions and shamanism.

Wicca seeks the development of psychic powers. Wicca generally worships the divine in two ways: the God and the Goddess. Nature is seen as sacred. Emphasizing a magick relation with the invisible world present all around us, rituals of the moon and the seasons help us to become aware of being part of the cosmos. The result is a better recognition of our body as it is and a harmonized life with the universe of which we are a part.

Eventually Wicca evolved into a large, worldwide movement composed of several groups, often influenced by their cultural background and the politics of their country.

I became interested in Wicca in the '80s. At that time, the only organization using the name Wicca in France was a Luciferian group totally different from the Wicca and the Covens we know in English-speaking countries. Consequently, in 1990, I created the first Wicca magazine (*Moïra*). Eventually I was initiated in the original form of this tradition.

Today Wicca remains a strong component of the Western tradition. The variety of existing Covens is proof of the power and the life of this spiritual heritage.

Ritual of the Wheel of the Year

Prayer beads are a recent contribution to Wicca. Wicca has always been a vibrant tradition, eager to incorporate useful symbols and ritual tools. In my practices outdoors, I began progressively to use prayer beads in order to improve some of the ritual invocations. They increase focus and help you maintain your level of consciousness. The beautiful aspect of such prayer beads is the possibility for you to keep them with you even in your daily life. There are not so many ritual tools you can carry with you wherever you go. Prayer beads are useful and at the same time they are a symbolic artwork you can wear proudly.

In Wicca, two fundamental aspects can be linked to create a very interesting ritual process: the wheel of the year and the four elements invoked when you create the sacred space.

The magick circle can be seen as the representation of the world. As a priest or a priestess, you are the one who recreates the cosmos and separates this sacred space from the common world. Understanding how the space is organized and divided helps us see the symbolic meaning of the ritual work.

Imagine that you are outside. On the Equinox, the sun rises exactly in the east and the sun sets in the west. It is easy then to find the two other directions (north and south) on the perpendicular axis. These four directions are associated to the four elements as follows: East—Air, South—Fire, West—Water, and North—Earth. The Solstices and Equinoxes are also symbolically associated to these directions: East—Spring Equinox, South—Summer Solstice, West—Fall Equinox, North—Winter Solstice. The reason is the simple observation of the movements of the sun during the year.

As you may know, eight celebrations compose the wheel of the year. In order to find the four other divisions, you only have to observe the sunrise and sunset on the two solstices. Then you obtain the beautiful symbolic representation of the octagon.

Purpose

This first ritual allows you to create a physical sacred space in which you will be able to perform meditations and rituals. It can also be performed mentally or in meditation in order to balance your inner elements and powers.

Description and Symbolism of Prayer Beads

These prayer beads summarize symbolically this wheel of the year and help us to invoke the power of the elements in the four compass points.

Prayer beads used in this ritual consist of a circle of thirty-two beads separated in four series of eight. The four series of beads are associated with the four directions. The number 8 connects each element to the whole cosmic representation in order to balance the power invoked.

The colors of the beads help you to visualize the energy involved. The colors of the four series correspond to the usual four colors of the elements in the Wicca tradition: green (Earth), yellow (Air), red (Fire), and blue (Water). Between each series is a separating bead, which is part of two central strings which constitute the axis of the wheel. One of these strings is for the God, and the other for the Goddess. One is made of eight green beads and the other of eight red beads. The symbol of the pentagram can be attached to the prayer beads.

Meditation

Light two candles, one for the Goddess (green or beeswax) and one for the God (red or beeswax).

Sit comfortably, take your prayer beads, and breathe peacefully a few minutes.

Then you can begin your meditation on the wheel of the year.

Even if a full cycle is enough to establish harmony in your visible and invisible bodies, I recommend performing three full cycles.

On the yellow series of beads, pronounce one time per bead, for a total of eight invocations:

O subtle creatures of the Air, O vibrant Sylphs, Elementals of the East, I invoke you!

Hear my call and help me to become the center of the wheel!

On the red series of beads, pronounce one time per bead, for a total of eight invocations:

O subtle creatures of the Fire, fiery salamander, Elementals of the South, I invoke you!

Hear my call and help me to become the center of the wheel!

On the blue series of beads, pronounce one time per bead, for a total of eight invocations:

O subtle creatures of the Water, graceful undines, Elementals of the West, I invoke you!

Hear my call and help me to become the center of the wheel!

On the green series of beads, pronounce one time per bead, for a total of eight invocations:

O subtle creatures of the Earth, powerful gnomes, Elementals of the North, I invoke you!

Hear my call and help me to become the center of the wheel!

On the axis series of red beads, pronounce one time per bead, for a total of eight invocations:

O Powerful God, I invoke you! Grant me your strength, joy, and life!

On the axis series of green beads, pronounce one time per bead, for a total of eight invocations:

O Powerful Goddess, I invoke you! Grant me your beauty, power, and wisdom!

Put your prayer beads in contact with the center of your chest and say:

Merry Meet, Merry Part, and Merry Meet Again!

Blessed be!

Individual Ritual
Tools

Prepare the sacred space as usual in the Wicca tradition. You can place an altar at the center. Two candles will be placed on it, one for the God and a second for the Goddess. The candle on the left side will be green and the other one on the right side will be red. If you cannot find these colors, don't worry and use beeswax instead. A cup of water will be on the left and a cup of salt on the right. Use water prepared as described in Chapter 3 of this book. It is good to have a pentacle represented in the middle of your altar. The prayer beads will be placed upon the pentagram. You can also use an athame[29] (a wooden dagger would be better[30]) even if this is not required.

A censer will be placed at the center of the altar, close to the east side.

You will draw the circle as it is taught in your tradition. If you have no specific indications, I recommend using a simple white cord to create a large circle on the floor around you. If you work alone, a diameter between 8' to 10' could be enough.

If you are working indoors, you can hang on the east wall the representation of the double square and the sun.[31]

Opening

Powers of the Elements

Light the candles beginning with the one dedicated to the Goddess.

Then take the cup of salt and, without moving from the place where you stand, project salt grains to the East, West, North, and South. Then replace the cup.

Take the cup of water and proceed in the same way.

Take the prayer beads in your right hand and go to the east of the circle, facing east. Then, using the eight yellow beads, pronounce eight times the invocation:

From the East where I stand, I invoke you, powers of the Air.

---

29. This is a small ritual dagger, which is usually composed of a double-edged blade and a black handle.
30. You can see several models at: www.theurgia.us.
31. A representation of this can be found on my website: www.debiasi.org.

May the breeze beginning to blow in the East manifest his presence.

O glorious beings that live in the infinite of the Air, hear my call! Come here and now!

Place the prayer beads on your finger as shown on the photo. The beads on the top of your fingers are the ones you just used for the invocation. Raise your hand in front of you, the right forefinger extended in direction to the east.

Using your forefinger as an athame, draw a pentagram of activation of the Element Air.

Release the position and go clockwise to the south of the circle, facing south.

Using the eight red beads, pronounce eight times the invocation:

From the South where I stand, I invoke you, powers of the Fire.

May the living flame rise in the South and manifest his presence!

O glorious beings that live in the infinite of the Fire, hear my call! Come here and now!

Take the same position you did for the previous direction and, using your forefinger as an athame, draw a pentagram of activation of the Element Fire.

Release the position and go clockwise to the west of the circle, facing west.

Using the eight blue beads, pronounce eight times the invocation:

From the West where I stand, I invoke you, powers of the Water.

May the falls, the springs, the lakes, the rivers, and the ocean flow in the West and manifest their presence!

O glorious beings that live in the infinite of the Water, hear my call! Come here and now!

Take the same position you did for the previous direction and using your forefinger as an athame, draw a pentagram of activation of the Element Water.

Release the position and go clockwise to the north of the circle, facing north.

Using the eight green beads, pronounce eight times the invocation:

From the North where I stand, I invoke you, powers of the Earth.

May the freshness of the depth of the earth emerge in the North and manifest his presence!

O glorious beings that live in the infinite of the earth, hear my call! Come here and now!

Take the same position you did for the previous direction and, using your forefinger as an athame, draw a pentagram of activation of the Element Earth.

Release the position and go clockwise to the east side of the altar.

Light the incense.

Building the Magical Circle

Your prayer beads in your left hand, the censer in your right hand, go to the east of the circle, staying inside it.

Draw a circle clockwise with the incense, visualizing a wall of light rising vertically from the cord. When you are back to the east, raise four times the censer to this direction, then move clockwise to the second point following the circle with the censer. Raise the incense again four times, and continue in the same way for the eight directions.[32] Visualize rays of pure light coming from these eight directions and connecting your sacred place to the high powers of the cosmos. The power of the place increases as the bright light becomes more present.

When you are back to the east, perform a third and last circle visualizing the same wall of light you did for the first circle.

When this circle is closed in the east, turn to your right, return to the altar, and replace the censer to its original place.

Calling the Directions

(If you use the athame in the following sequence, you will trace the pentagram with the athame instead of your forefinger.)

---

32. You can follow the indications found on my website: www.debiasi.org.

Take your prayer beads in your right hand and come back to the east point of the circle, facing east.

Open your arms and say:

O subtle creatures of the Air, O vibrant Sylphs, Elementals of the East, I invoke you!

Be welcomed in this sacred circle!

Help me in the Great Work I am about to begin!

Pronounce this invocation eight times, each time on a yellow bead.

Then draw the same pentagram you used previously for this direction with your forefinger and the prayer beads, just as you did in the first part.

Put your finger on the separating bead and go to the south. During your walk, repeat the vowel "**A.**"

Face south. Open your arms and say:

O subtle creatures of the Fire, fiery Salamanders, Elementals of the South, I invoke you!

Be welcomed in this sacred circle!

Help me in the Great Work I am about to begin!

Pronounce this invocation eight times, each time on a red bead.

Then proceed as you did for the previous direction.

When you are facing the west, your arms open, say:

O subtle creatures of the Water, graceful Undines, Elementals of the West, I invoke you!

Be welcomed in this sacred circle!

Help me in the Great Work I am about to begin!

Pronounce this invocation eight times, each time on a blue bead.

Then proceed as you did for the previous direction.

When you are facing the north, your arms open, say:

O subtle creatures of the Earth, powerful Gnomes, Elementals of the North, I invoke you!

Be welcomed in this sacred circle!

Help me in the Great Work I am about to begin!

Pronounce this invocation eight times, each time on a green bead.

Then go to the west of the altar, facing east, and kneel. Meditate a few minutes in silence.

Take the candle of the God in your right hand. Visualize the presence of the God in front of the altar. Your eyes are closed or half-open. Using the red axis of your prayer beads, repeat eight times:

Powerful God, I welcome you in this sacred circle!

Replace the candle.

Take the candle of the Goddess in your right hand and proceed with the green axis as you did previously. Repeat eight times this invocation:

Powerful Goddess, I welcome you in this sacred circle!

Replace the candle and the prayer beads.

Meditation

Stay where you are and spend a few minutes in adoration or meditation, feeling the presence of the invisible powers all around you.

When you feel that you can close the circle, stand up, facing the east.

Closing

Blessing of the Divinities

Direct your hands to the candles. The left palm is in direction to the candle of the Goddess and the right palm in direction to the candle of the God. Keeping this position, say:

O Powerful Goddess, I thank you for your presence in this sacred circle.

As you leave this place, grant me a part of your beauty, power, and wisdom!

O Powerful God, I thank you for your presence in this sacred circle.

As you leave this place, grant me a part of your strength, joy, and life!

Greetings to the Elemental Powers

Take the prayer beads and go to the north, facing north.
Open your arms and say:

O subtle creatures of the Earth, powerful Gnomes, Elementals of the North, I thank you for your presence and your support in this ritual!

I salute you as you return to your world!

Then draw the pentagram of deactivation of the Earth with your forefinger still holding the the prayer beads in your hand.
Go to the west and proceed as you did in the north, saying:

O subtle creatures of the Water, powerful Undines, Elementals of the West, I thank you for your presence and your support in this ritual!

I salute you as you return to your world!

Then draw the pentagram of deactivation of Water with your forefinger still holding the the prayer beads in your hand.
Go to the south and proceed as you did in the north, saying:

O subtle creatures of the Fire, powerful Salamanders, Elementals of the South, I thank you for your presence and your support in this ritual!

I salute you as you return to your world!

Then draw the pentagram of deactivation of the Fire with your forefinger, still holding the the prayer beads in your hand.

Go to the east and proceed as you did in the north, saying:

O subtle creatures of the Air, powerful Sylphs, Elementals of the East, I thank you for your presence and your support in this ritual!

I salute you as you return to your world!

Then draw the pentagram of deactivation of the Air with your forefinger, still holding the prayer beads in your hand.

Release of the Circle

As you are in the east of the circle, perform three circumambulations counterclockwise. The prayer beads are in your left hand and your right hand is open, palm down at the vertical of the cord. With the help of your visualization you will dissolve the walls of light. During this walk counterclockwise, you can repeat on each bead the words:

Blessed be!

It is not necessary here to count. Just stop using the prayer beads when the three circumambulations are achieved.

Blessings of the Worlds

Come back to the west of the altar, facing east, replace the prayer beads on the altar, and say:

Powers of Earth and Fire, I thank you for your support in the magical work I just achieved.

May the harmony created between you and me continue to grow every day!

I salute you as you leave this place!

Powers of Air and Water, I thank you for your support in the magical work I just achieved.

May the harmony created between you and me continue to grow every day!

I salute you as you leave this place!

After few seconds of silence, say:

The circle is open!

Merry Meet, Merry Part, and Merry Meet Again!

Blessed be!

Two-person Ritual

One will be the Priest and the other one will be the Priestess. Remember that a couple is just an assembly of two persons regardless of gender or relationship status. Consequently, my use of the terms "Priest" and "Priestess" must be just considered as an easy way to characterize the invisible power involved.

Organization of the Place

Prepare the sacred place as you did for the individual ritual. You will add a cup of wine and a cup for the libations if you are working indoors.

Opening

Powers of the Elements

Light the candles, beginning with the one dedicated to the Goddess.

The Priest takes the cup of salt and, without moving from the place where he stands, projects salt grains to the East, West, North, and South. Then the Priest replaces the cup.

The Priestess takes the cup of water and proceeds in the same way.

Both take their prayer beads in their right hands.

The Priestess goes to the east of the circle and the Priest to the west of the circle. She faces the Priest. She bows for a few seconds in his direction, rises and faces the East. Then using the eight yellow beads, she pronounces the invocation eight times:

From the East where I stand, I invoke you, powers of the Air.

May the breeze begin to blow in the East and manifest his presence.

O glorious beings that live in the infinite of the Air, hear my call! Come, here and now!

She goes clockwise to the north of the circle. The Priest goes clockwise to the south. He bows for a few seconds in her direction, rises and faces the South.

Using the eight red beads, he pronounces the invocation eight times:

From the South where I stand, I invoke you, powers of the Fire.

May the living flame rise in the South and manifest his presence!

O glorious beings that live in the infinite of the Fire, hear my call! Come, here and now!

The Priest goes clockwise to the east of the circle and the Priestess goes clockwise to the west of the circle. She faces the Priest. She bows for a few seconds in his direction, rises, and faces the West.

Using the eight blue beads, she pronounces the invocation eight times:

From the West where I stand, I invoke you, powers of the Water.

May the falls, springs, lakes, rivers, and the ocean flow in the West and manifest their presence!

O glorious beings that live in the infinite of the Water, hear my call! Come, here and now!

She goes clockwise to the south of the circle. The Priest goes to the north. He bows for a few seconds in her direction, rises, and faces the North.

Using the eight green beads, he pronounces the invocation eight times:

From the North where I stand, I invoke you, powers of the Earth.

May the freshness of the depth of the earth emerge in the North and manifest his presence!

O glorious beings that live in the infinite of the Earth, hear my call! Come, here and now!

He goes clockwise to the west of the circle. The Priestess goes to the east.

The Priest steps to the west of the altar, facing east.

The Priestess steps to the east of the altar, facing west and the Priest.

Both replace their prayer beads. The Priest lights the incense.

Building the Magical Circle

The Priestess takes the censer in her right hand, and goes to the east of the circle, staying inside it.

She draws a circle clockwise with the incense, visualizing a wall of light rising from the cord. When she is back to the east, she raises the censer four times to this direction, then moves clockwise to the second point following the circle with the censer, raises the incense again four times, and continues in the same way for the eight directions. Both of them visualize rays of pure light coming from these eight directions and connecting this sacred place to the high powers of the cosmos. This magical connection creates a real increase of bright light in the room.

When she is back to the east, she performs a third and last circle, visualizing the same wall of light she did for the first circle.

When this circle is closed in the east, she turns to her right to face the altar and approaches it to replace the censer in its original place. Then both of them take their prayer beads in their right hands.

Calling the Directions

The Priestess and the Priest will call the directions following the same five positions on the circle they did for the first part of this ritual, called "Powers of the Elements."

Priestess (to the east)

Arms opened, she says:

O subtle creatures of the Air, O vibrant Sylphs, Elementals of the East, I invoke you!

Be welcomed in this sacred circle!

Help me in the Great Work which I am about to begin!

She pronounces this invocation eight times, each time on a yellow bead.

Then she draws the pentagram of the element in activation, the prayer beads on her finger as it was described in the individual ritual.

Priest (to the South)

Arms opened, he says:

O subtle creatures of the Fire, fiery Salamanders, Elementals of the South, I invoke you!

Be welcomed in this sacred circle!

Help me in the Great Work I am about to begin!

He pronounces this invocation eight times, each time on a red bead.

Then he draws the pentagram of the element in activation, the prayer beads on his finger as described previously.

Priestess (to the west)

Arms opened, she says:

O subtle creatures of the Water, graceful Undines, Elementals of the West, I invoke you!

Be welcomed in this sacred circle!

Help me in the Great Work I am about to begin!

She pronounces this invocation eight times, each time on a blue bead.

Then she draws the pentagram of the element in activation, the prayer beads on her finger as described previously.

Priest (to the north)

Arms opened, he says:

O subtle creatures of the Earth, powerful Gnomes, Elementals of the North, I invoke you!

Be welcomed in this sacred circle!

Help me in the Great Work I am about to begin!

He pronounces this invocation eight times, each time on a green bead.

Then he draws the pentagram of the element in activation, the prayer beads on his finger as described previously.

Moving clockwise, the Priest goes to the south of the altar facing north, and the Priestess to the north of the altar, facing south.

Both take the candle in their left hands, the prayer beads being in their right hands.

Both meditate for a few seconds in silence.

The Priestess visualizes the Priest as the manifestation of the God. Eyes half-opened and using the red axis of her prayer beads, she repeats eight times:

Powerful God, I welcome you in this sacred circle!

The Priest visualizes the Priestess as the manifestation of the Goddess. Eyes half-opened and using the green axis of his prayer beads, he repeats eight times:

Powerful Goddess, I welcome you in this sacred circle!

After few seconds of silence, both replace the candles and their prayer beads on the altar.

Anointment

Both go to the west side of the altar.

The Priest puts oil on his thumb, raises his arms in the direction of the Priestess, and says:

I recognize you as the incarnation of the Goddess.

Then he traces the symbol of the circled cross on the forehead of the Priestess, saying at the same time:

May your power be now fully manifested!

The priest bends over the Priestess for a few seconds.

The Priestess does the same. Then, her arms open, she says:

I recognize you as the incarnation of the God.

Then she traces the symbol of the circled cross on the forehead of the Priest, saying at the same time:

May your power be now fully manifested!

The Priestess bends over the Priest for a few seconds.

The Priest takes the cup of wine and pours few drops into the cup of libation, saying:

May the multiple manifestations of the Goddess be honored!

Then he gives the cup to the Priestess, saying:

Be honored, Goddess, and accept this beverage as the manifestation of my love for you!

The Priestess drinks some of the wine.

After few seconds of silence, the Priestess pours a few drops in the cup of libation, saying:

May the multiple manifestations of the God be honored!

Then she gives the cup to the Priest, saying:

Be honored, God, and accept this beverage as the manifestation of my love for you!

The Priest drinks some of the wine and replaces the cup on the altar.

Meditation or Psychic Work

During this time, you can sit face-to-face, keeping in you the presence of the God and the Goddess. It is a good idea to work together on your inner energy and any other psychic work.

You can also practice during this time the rituals of the God and Goddess found later in this chapter.

When you feel it is time to close the circle, stand up, facing the east.

Closing

Blessing of the Divinities

Priest and Priestess are face-to-face. The Priest looks the Priestess in the eyes and says:

O Powerful Goddess, I thank you for your presence in this sacred circle.

The Priest bows before the Priestess. The Priestess puts her hands on the head of the Priest and says:

Before I leave this place, I give you beauty, power, and wisdom!

Both release their position and stay a few seconds in silence.

Then the Priestess looks the Priest in the eyes and says:

O Powerful God, I thank you for your presence in this sacred circle.

Then the Priestess bows before the Priest. The Priest puts his hands on the head of the Priestess and says:

Before I leave this place, I give you strength, joy, and life!

Both release their position and stay a few seconds in silence.

Greetings to the Elemental Powers

Priest and Priestess will proceed as they did for the opening, but this time moving counterclockwise.

1. Priest facing north (Priestess is in the south), opens his arms and says:

O subtle creatures of the Earth, powerful Gnomes, Elementals of the North, I thank you for your presence and your support in this ritual!

I salute you as you return to your world!

Then he draws the pentagram of deactivation of Earth with his forefinger, still holding the the prayer beads in his hand.

2. Priestess facing west (Priest is in the east), opens her arms and says:

O subtle creatures of the Water, powerful Undines, Elementals of the West, I thank you for your presence and your support in this ritual!

I salute you as you return to your world!

Then she draws the pentagram of deactivation of Water with her forefinger, still holding the the prayer beads in her hand.

3. Priest facing south (Priestess in the north), opens his arms and says:

O subtle creatures of the Fire, powerful Salamanders, Elementals of the South, I thank you for your presence and your support in this ritual!

I salute you as you return to your world!

Then he draws the pentagram of deactivation of Fire with his forefinger, still holding the the prayer beads in his hand.

4. Priestess facing east (Priest is in the west), opens her arms and says:

O subtle creatures of the Air, powerful Sylphs, Elementals of the East, I thank you for your presence and your support in this ritual!

I salute you as you return to your world!

Then she draws the pentagram of deactivation of Air with her forefinger, still holding the the prayer beads in her hand.

Release of the Circle

Priestess goes to the west of the altar and faces east. The Priest goes to the east of the circle and from this point performs three circumambulations counterclockwise. His prayer beads are in his left hand and his right hand is open, palm down, at the vertical axis of the cord. With the help of his visualization he dissolves the walls of light. During this walk counterclockwise, he can repeat on each bead the words:

Blessed be!

He stops using the prayer beads when the three circumambulations are achieved.

Blessings of the Worlds

The Priest comes back to the west of the altar, faces east, replaces the prayer beads on the altar, and says:

Powers of Earth and Fire, I thank you for your support in the magical work I just achieved.

May the harmony created between us continue to grow every day!

I salute you as you leave this place!

The Priestess says:

Powers of Air and Water, I thank you for your support in the magical work I just achieved.

May the harmony created between us continue to grow every day!

I salute you as you leave this place!

After a few seconds of silence, both say:

The circle is open!

Merry Meet, Merry Part, and Merry Meet Again!

Blessed be!

GROUP RITUAL
Process

The process is the same as for the practice for a couple. Remember that the participants must remain inside the circle at all times.

When invocations are pronounced by the Priest and the Priestess during the "Powers of the Elements" and "Calling the Directions," everyone can use their own prayer beads and repeat the same words at the same time.

During the time of meditation and psychic work, everyone can participate.

Ritual of the Goddess

Undoubtedly the Goddess is the main focus of the Wiccan tradition. In the pre-Christian times the gender of the deities was not a problem per se. It was natural for all believers to see representations of Gods and Goddesses side by side. It was common to worship a Goddess in her temple and to go a few minutes later to another temple or shrine dedicated to a God. However, after centuries of destruction, cults of the Goddess were eradicated. Of course their presences were maintained in different ways. In the southwest of France, where I was born, several churches possess ancient statues of black virgins. Most of the time, their representations are the same as the statues of Isis in ancient Egypt. Stories often tell how these statues were found in the ground, sometimes in the center of a wheel. Their discoveries are often related to miracles. They were the center of popular cults and pilgrimages, even if the churches were small and hidden in the country.

It is also interesting to see that such statues were found in special places that all constitute symbolic figures in the geography of the land. For example, we can see such statues in five different chapels. When you take a map and observe the position of these chapels, they are all exactly on the same line. It is clear that such locations are not random and that they show a perception of lines of power in the ground. We are not so far from the symbolic and geographical representation of a string of prayer beads.

Don't be fooled by the presence of such divinities in Catholic churches. They were placed at the most convenient place of the time: churches. It is important to keep in mind that in order to maintain the invisible power of divinities, it is necessary that their cult continues. Sometimes the details of their representation can vary slightly without changing anything as a result. However, the theology associated with the "black virgin Mary" is very different from the theology of the Goddess worshipped by Wiccans. The real Goddess has nothing to do with Christianity. The text of the Bible itself is enough to understand how far the women are from being considered as Goddesses. So yes, you can still see in France and elsewhere in Europe such ancient statues, but keep in mind that they are not well-surrounded with the omnipresence of male domination. Such is not an adequate place for a well-balanced cult.

Every time I find myself in front of such a statue, I strongly wish that it were possible to move it and put it on a rocky altar under the full moon. Then, I would be sure that the statue could breathe at last!

Purpose

This ritual will be used to worship the Goddess under her lunar manifestation. No matter if you are a man or a woman, invoking the divine powers of the moon will give you balance and increase your deep relation with the mysteries of nature. You will be able to connect faster with the elements and rebuild your energies faster when you need it.

Description and Symbolism of the Prayer Beads

Four different prayer beads can be used for this ritual:

1. The first one represents symbolically the full lunar cycle. This is a circle of twenty-eight beads separated in four series of seven. The four series of beads are associated to the four

moon phases. The number 28 (2+8) can be reduced to the number 10, which represents two important things:

a) The shape of the numbers represents the symbolic union between the male and female (I—O);

b) The number 10 represents the divine Tetraktys, the four elements,[33] and the harmony of the cosmos.

The colors of the four series correspond to the progression of the Moon: white, black, and grey. Between each phase you can find four charms, which represent these moon phases.

Use: These prayer beads can be used at any time of the phase of the moon.

2. The second one corresponds to the new moon. This is also a circle of the same number of beads. They are all black. Between each series you can find four charms, which represent the new moon.

Use: It's best to use these prayer beads between "Waxing Crescent" and "Waning Crescent."

3. The third one corresponds to the first and third quarters of the moon. This is also a circle of the same number of beads. They are all grey. Between each series you can find four charms, which represent the crescent moon.

Use: It's best to use these prayer beads during two periods: 1. Between "Waxing Gibbous" and "Waxing Crescent"; 2. Between "Waning Crescent" and "Waning Gibbous."

---

33. A representation can be found on my website: www.debiasi.org.

4. The fourth one corresponds to the full moon. This is a circle of twenty-eight beads separated in four series of seven. All the beads are white. Between each series you can find four charms, which represent the full moon.

Use: It's best to use these prayer beads, between "Waning Gibbous" and "Waxing Gibbous."

Meditation

Light two candles, one for the Goddess (green or beeswax) and one for the God (red or beeswax).

Sit comfortably, take your prayer beads and breathe peacefully for a few minutes.

Remember that you can perform this lunar meditation on its own or integrate it in the previous meditation on the wheel of the year. In this case you will begin by the previous one and then continue with this one.

Meditation on the Full Cycle of the Moon

This meditation can be performed at any moment of the cycle of the moon in order to increase your connection with the power of the moon and improve your intuition.

1. Take the first prayer beads described previously, which correspond to the full moon cycle (twenty-eight beads/four series of seven/black, grey, white).

Begin by the symbol of the new moon. Keep this charm between your thumb and your forefinger, then focus on the presence of the Goddess Hekate. Breathe regularly and declaim the orphic hymn to this Goddess:

O Hekate, loving and desirable Goddess, you who protect the roads and crossroads, I invoke you!

The safran color of your peplos manifests your presence to the Souls wandering in obscurity.

You, watcher of the skies, the Earth, and the seas, daughter of Perseus, incomparable huntress, I salute you!

Terrifying Queen of the night, you love dogs, and the sound of animals announces your presence.

You are the Supreme Guardian of the Cosmos who watches over the sacred bulls.

You, who are the guide, and the nurse of young men, hearken and be present as I celebrate this sacred rite!

Rejoice in my offering of incense! Be favorable to me, and grant me success!

Then on each of the seven following black beads, pronounce (or sing):

Hekate, be favorable to me and grant me your powers to succeed!

2. Take the following charm of the crescent moon between your thumb and your forefinger, then declaim the orphic hymn to Artemis:

Hearken, O Artemis, daughter of Zeus of the thousand names, roaring Titan of illustrious name, holy archer, you whose glittering torches illuminate us, O Dictynna!

Although not initiated to these mysteries, you protect those who give birth and appease the pains of child-birth.

O you who unite desires, friend of holy delirium, you who hunt with dogs and dissipate sorrows, hear my words.

You who hunt in the night, running swiftly, shooting arrows,

You whose subtle and virile form captivates my gaze,

You who welcome, free, and bring renown,

You, Orthia, Goddess of quick childbirth, nurse of young men, answer to my calling!

O venerable Immortal and terrestrial, killer of felines, you reign on mountainous forests! Holy and absolute Queen, beautiful and imperishable flower, you dwell in

deep and mysterious woods, you who like dogs, Kydo-
nian of changing forms!

Come, saving Goddess, loving, kind to every initiate,
and give me the beautiful fruits of the Earth, desirable
peace, and good health.

Hunt on the peaks of mountains every ill and suffering!

O Artemis, holy huntress, be with me at this instant!

Then on each of the seven following grey beads, pronounce
(or sing):

Artemis, give me the beautiful fruits of the Earth, desirable peace, and good health!

3. Take the following charm of the full moon between your
thumb and your forefinger; then declaim the orphic hymn to
Selene:

Hearken, O Divine Queen!

Powerful Selene, shine forth on this place!

You, who encircle the night and manifest your presence in the surrounding air, be among us!

You, maiden of the night, torch-bearer, magnificent star, waxing and waning, male and female, mother of time;

You, glittering silver light of the night, turn your gaze on us and our works.

Splendid vestment of night, bestow upon us your grace and perfection.

May your celestial course guide you towards us, O wise maiden.

Come, you who are the most joyful of all! Be propitious and shine your lights on this new initiate in all three of your aspects.

Then on each of the seven following white beads, pronounce (or sing):

Selene, wise Goddess, grant me the power of magick and intuition!

4. Take the following charm of the crescent moon between your thumb and your forefinger; then declaim the same orphic hymn to Artemis you previously used. Use also the same declamation for the seven grey beads.

5. Take the following charm of the new moon between your thumb and your forefinger.

Then declaim (or sing) one time each of the sacred names of the Goddesses:

Hekate, Artemis, Selene.

Breathe, relax; put your prayer beads in contact with the center of your chest and say:

May the powers of the Goddesses be a living part of myself!

Blessed be!

Meditation on the First Cycle of the Moon to Hekate

The best period for this meditation is between "Waxing Crescent" and "Waning Crescent." Use the previously described set of beads that are all black.

Use the hymn and invocation of Hekate provided in the previous part.

On each charm, pronounce the full hymn to the Goddess and the invocations on the beads. Your meditation will be composed of four pronunciations of the hymn and twenty-eight invocations.

If you want to deepen your contact with this specific Goddess, you can perform three full cycles, one for each aspect of the Goddess. If you decide to go with this triple cycle, I suggest you change the names for the invocations.

During the first cycle you will say on each of the twenty-eight beads:

Foïbiê, be favorable to me and grant me your powers to succeed!

During the second cycle, say on each of the twenty-eight beads:

Dionê, be favorable to me and grant me your powers to succeed!

During the third cycle, say on each of the twenty-eight beads:

Nukhiê, be favorable to me and grant me your powers to succeed!

The hymns used on the separating beads are the same as before.

Individual Ritual
Tools

Prepare the sacred space as you did for the first ritual of this chapter. If you have the time to perform the full ritual, I recommend integrating this ritual during the "Meditation" time of the "Ritual of the Wheel of the Year."

Besides the tools needed for the latter, take the lunar prayer beads you want to use in your practice. It could be good to also use lunar incense and oil.

Opening

Follow the "Ritual of the Wheel of the Year" until the meditation period.

Take a time to relax and breathe.

Lunar Invocation

1. Use of the first prayer beads of the full lunar cycle

Take your prayer beads.

In this case, I will describe the way to use the first prayer beads about the full lunar cycle.

Take your lunar oil and anoint the part of your hand shown on the representation opposite.

Light your incense. Take the censer in your left hand and the prayer beads in your right hand.

West: Stand up and go to the west of the circle, facing this direction.

Begin by the symbol of the new moon. Keeping this charm between your thumb and your forefinger, focus on the presence of the Goddess Hekate you visualize in front of you.

Raise the censer three times in the direction of the Goddess.

Breathe regularly and declaim the orphic hymn to this Goddess as you did in the previous meditation.

Place the censer on the floor.

Use the first series of the black beads as you did in the previous part. When you have achieved the seven invocations to Hekate, wind the prayer beads on your hand. Raise your arm to the west and vibrate (or sing) one time while drawing a circle clockwise, beginning by the top of it.

North: Take the censer and go to the north of the circle, facing this direction. Proceed in the same way with the Goddess Artemis, her hymn, and the invocation on the gray beads. (Raise the censer four times.)

Draw the symbol of the crescent.

East: Take the censer and go to the east of the circle, facing this direction. Proceed in the same way with the Goddess Selene, her hymn, and the invocation on the white beads. (Raise the censer four times.)

Draw a circle clockwise beginning by the top of it.

South: Take the censer and go to the south of the circle, facing this direction. Proceed in the same way with the Goddess Artemis, her hymn, and the invocation on the gray beads. (Raise the censer four times.)

Draw the symbol of the crescent.

Take the censer and come back to the west to close the circle. Then go in front of your altar, replace the prayer beads, and meditate.

When you feel the time is right, close the ritual in the same way as the "Ritual of the Wheel of the Year."

2. Use of the other lunar prayer beads

It is good to perform this ritual at the different phases of the moon.

Proceed in the same way as you just did for the previous ritual. The only adaptations are the following:

• Begin by the direction of the period of the moon in which you are working.

- Use the same hymn and invocation in the different directions without consideration of the attributions you previously used.

- Use the specific oil and incense for the divinity if this is convenient for you.

Two-person Ritual

One will be the Priest and the other one will be the Priestess.

Organization of the Place

Proceed in the same way you did for the ritual for the couple in the wheel of the year.

This ritual for the couple is performed during the meditation part.

1. Use of the first prayer beads of the full lunar cycle

East: The Priestess takes the lunar oil and goes to the west of the circle, facing east.

The Priest takes the censer in his left hand and his prayer beads in the right hand. He goes in front of her and kneels in silence.

The Priestess meditates on the Goddess Hekate and welcomes her into her body. The Priestess progressively becomes the manifestation of the Goddess as the Priest begins to declaim the hymn followed by the seven invocations.

At the end of these invocations, the Priestess/Goddess draws with the oil a circle clockwise on the forehead of the Priest. Then she puts her hands on the head of the Priest and says:

May your desire be fulfilled!

Blessed Be!

North: The Priest stands up. The Priestess goes to the north of the circle, facing south. The Priest goes to be in front of her.

Follow the same process you just did in the west. The manifestation of the Goddess is in this case Artemis. The symbol drawn with the oil is the crescent of the moon.

East: Proceed in the same way as before. The manifestation of the Goddess is in this case Selene. The symbol drawn with the oil is the circle clockwise of the moon.

South: Proceed in the same way as before. The manifestation of the Goddess is in this case Artemis. The symbol drawn with the oil is the crescent of the moon.

Complete the circle in the west and come back in front of the altar, replace all the tools used, and meditate.

When you feel the time is right, close the ritual in the same way as the "Ritual of the Wheel of the Year."

2. Use of the other lunar prayer beads
It is good to perform this ritual at the different phases of the moon.

Proceed in the same way as you just did for the previous ritual. The only adaptations are the following:

- Begin by the direction of the period of the moon in which you are working.
- The Priestess manifests the same aspect of the lunar divinity all along the ritual.

- The Priest uses the same hymn and invocation in the different directions without consideration of the attributions previously used.

- Use the specific oil and incense for the divinity if this is convenient for you.

GROUP RITUAL
Process

The group ritual uses the opening and closing of the "Ritual of the Wheel of the Year."

In the central part dedicated to the lunar work, all the participants move with the Priest and are doing the same thing he is doing regarding the hymns and invocations. However, he is the only one to raise the incense.

When the Priestess anoints the forehead of the Priest, she moves in front of each participant to do the same. When this is done, she goes to the next direction.

Ritual of the God

It has always been strange to me to talk about "God" in the case of the Wiccan or Pagan tradition. This oddness doesn't really exist for the "Goddess." Spontaneously we know that she can be manifested in different ways. However, for the "God" this is not so obvious. Due to 1,500 years of monotheistic tradition, the word "God" has come to express the "unique God revealed in the Bible." This is "God—father." Of course you know, and everyone knows, that this was an extension of a tribal Mediterranean God who progressively conquered the whole world. That doesn't mean he was and still is

the only one. We have to keep in mind that there is a difference between a divine principle we can call "Supreme Being"
or "God" and specific divinities such as, for example, "Helios,"
"Thoth," or "Yahweh."

When Christianity began to expand under the influence of
Paul, a strong castration was implemented. The goal was to
cut all other appearances of Gods in order to keep the unique
one "Yahweh" and to reduce the "Supreme divine principle" to
that mold. Then this original Hebrew figure was modified to
integrate a few other aspects needed to monopolize and control the whole religious world: a hero (half God, half human),
Jesus; a virgin (only devoted to God and capable of giving
birth), Mary; and a pure spirit (messenger and manifestation
of God), the Holy Spirit. Even if you keep just one of these
three aspects, you still obtain the absolute power of a male figure, which has eliminated all the other Immortal Divinities. If
you read about what happened from a political point of view,
it is what is called a "coup d'état." The result was uncertain at
the beginning but eventually worked. Our civilization is the
heir of this general castration.

This is what we have to keep in mind when we talk about
"God." Even if you are talking about the "God" in Wicca, even
if you know that God is as multiple as the Goddess is, you
have to know that powerful unbalanced egregores were built
from this male divine representation. This is why polytheism
is an essential key to tolerance. If we accept the idea that Gods
are multiple and immortal, then any monopoly will appear as
it is: a simple political power.

For a very short time I was involved very closely with the Christian priesthood. There are things you cannot learn intellectually. You have to feel them from the deepest part of your soul. That is the only way. There are truths related to their power that any Christian priest will keep secret. As this is not the subject of this book, I will only mention here the arrogance of the clergy to claim they possess the absolute and final truth of the universe. When they had that absolute certainty, they did one single thing: convince or impose their opinion on anyone and declare all other ways to see the divine as false. Even if the discourse can be adjusted to the present time, the inner certainty and the goal stay the same: monopoly.

Wicca and Paganism have a different goal, which is quite the opposite: multiplicity and tolerance! Working in this spirit, you can invoke the God you want or need. You can also change. The Wicca tradition is very much focused on the cycles of nature and everything related to it. For the Goddess, I chose to give you a practice related to the Moon and to Greek manifestations of the Moon Goddess. Following that logic, I chose the Sun as manifestation of the God. Then I used the Egyptian pantheon to connect with this very ancient divine power.

Purpose

This ritual will be used to worship the God under his solar manifestation. No matter if you are a man or a woman, invoking the divine powers of the Sun will give you balance and increase your deep relation with the energy of life present in nature. You will be able to use more efficiently your inner energies and easily increase your solar center when you need it. Worshipping these various God forms with the use of the prayer beads will help you to connect with the pre-Christian tradition.

Description and Symbolism of the Prayer Beads

Two different prayer beads can be used for this ritual:

1. The first one represents symbolically the daily solar cycle. This is a circle of twenty-four beads separated in four series of six. The four series of beads are associated with the four solar phases. Two colors of beads manifest the night hours and the daylight hours: white and deep blue.

Two separating beads show midnight and midday. Two separating beads indicate the sunset and sunrise. These four beads are golden.

The number 24 symbolizes the full cycle of the day. The addition of these two numbers, 2 and 4, gives a total of 6, which can be represented by the union of the two triangles, balance of the four elements.

2. The second one corresponds to the annual cycle of the sun. This is a circle composed of forty-eight beads. Twelve groups of three beads correspond to the astrological signs. They are all separated by golden beads. The color of the thirty-six beads is deep blue.

Use: These two sets of prayer beads can be used any day of the year.

Meditation

Light two candles, one for the Goddess (green or beeswax) and one for the God (red or beeswax).

Sit comfortably, take your prayer beads, and breathe peace-fully for a few minutes.

Remember that, as for the lunar meditation, you can per-form it on its own or integrate it in the previous meditation on the wheel of the year. In this case you will begin by the pre-vious one and then continue with this one.

Prayer Bead of the Day

First Meditation

Take the first prayer beads described previously correspond-ing to the daily solar cycle (twenty-four beads/four series of six/four separating golden beads) in your right hand and stand up in front of the east.

Open your arms, breathe in silence, and declaim the fol-lowing invocation:

I searched in the sky, I dug in the horizon, and I trav-elled the Earth in all directions to find the legacy of my elders.

I know all the secrets of creation, and the place where stands the crew of Ra's sacred bark.

I know the rebirths of Ra and his transformations in the deep waters.

I know the one who is in the bark of the day and in the bark of the night.

O Amon Ra, Master of the Horizon, gather your scattered limbs, and from the deepest darkness hear the praises of the crew of your bark and of the worshippers.

O Amon Ra, awake! You are the victorious One piloting the bark that carries light to the world.

O Amon Ra, arise, foster justice and destroy iniquity.

Breathe in silence and sit.

Take the first golden bead beginning the series of the day. Keeping your thumb and finger on it, declaim the sunrise adoration:

Hail unto thee, Khepera, in thy rising!

Hail unto thee, Heru-Khuti Khepera,[34] creator of thine own manifestation!

When thou art in the bark of the morning, the winds rejoice thy heart.

At the limits of day, thy beauty is before me, O living Lord, and my soul proclaims that thou art my lord forever.

Hail unto thee, Khepera, in thy rising!

---

34. Pronunciation (from the Hebrew chart): airoo kooti kaipaira.

Heru-Khuti Khepera, hail unto thee!

One time on each of the six following beads, declaim:

Heru-Khuti Khepera, hail unto thee!

Take the second golden bead beginning the second series of the day. Keeping your thumb and finger on it, declaim the noon adoration:

Hail unto thee, Amon Ra, on this resplendent day!

Hail unto thee, Heru-Khuti Ra, Master of the Gods!

When thou art in thy bark above the skies, thy spreading golden light rejoices thy heart.

At the zenith of the day, thy beauty is without parallel, O living Lord, and my soul proclaims that thou art my lord forever.

Hail unto thee, Amon Ra, on this resplendent day!

Heru-Khuti Amon Ra, hail unto thee!

One time on each of the six following beads, declaim:

Heru-Khuti Amon Ra, hail unto thee!

Take the third golden bead beginning the first series of the night. Keeping your thumb and finger on it, declaim the sunset adoration:

Hail unto thee, Temu, beautiful in thy setting!

Temu Heru-Khuti,[35] thy rays are splendid to mine eyes!

When thou dost proceed in the bark of the evening, the wandering stars chant to thee, and the sentinel stars utter praises unto thee.

At the limits of day, thy beauty is before me, O living Lord, and my soul proclaims that thou art my Lord forever.

Hail unto thee, Temu, in thy setting!

Temu Heru-Khuti, hail unto thee!

One time on each of the six following beads, declaim:

Temu Heru-Khuti, hail unto thee!

Take the fourth golden bead, beginning the second series of the night. Keeping your thumb and finger on it, declaim the midnight adoration:

---

35. Pronunciation (from the Hebrew chart): taimoo hairoo kooti.

Hail unto thee, in thy hiding!

Thy rays have withdrawn from the world.

As thy bark proceeds pausely through the deep night, the wandering stars ever glorify thee. The sentinel stars utter praises unto thee.

In the deepest night, thou concealst thy beauty, O living Lord, and my soul proclaims that thou art my lord forever.

Hail unto thee, in thy hiding!

O Immortal God, hail unto thee!

One time on each of the six following beads, declaim:

O Immortal God, hail unto thee!

Stand up and, raising your arms in direction to the sky, say:

Hail unto thee, O Amon-Ra, the sacred falcon who delights the land with beauty!

Thou flyest across the sky, traversing the earth and defeating the evil serpent!

**I praise thee, O King of Eternity, thou who overturn
his enemies and illumine the sanctuary of his adorers!**

Exalted art thou, O Ra!

Good art thou, O Ra!

Powerful art thou!

Beloved art thou, O Ra!

Well-watered art thou, O Ra!

Satisfied art thou, O Ra!

Free art thou, O Ra!

Second Meditation

I personally use this second meditation when I have enough
time to deepen the contact with the solar power.

The process will be divided in four parts, each one being
associated to one of the four separations of the day.

1. Sunrise (or when you wake up):

If you can, face east. Take your prayer beads and begin by
the golden bead that separates the beads of the night and the
beads of the day.

Declaim the sunrise adoration. (You can find it in the first
meditation).

Then, begin by the first white beads series and one time on each of the six following beads, declaim:

Heru-Khuti Khepera, hail unto thee!

You will continue to use the same adoration (on the golden beads) and invocation (on the white and deep blue beads) in order to use the full prayer beads. The total of your adorations will be four, and of your invocations, twenty-four.

2. Midday:

If you can, face south. Proceed as you did for sunrise. The adoration and invocation are indicated in the first meditation. Begin by the golden bead, which symbolizes midday.

3. Sunset:

If you can, face west. Proceed as you did for sunrise. The adoration and invocation are indicated in the first meditation. Begin by the golden bead, which symbolizes the sunset.

4. Midnight (or few minutes before going to bed):

If you can, face north. Proceed as you did for sunrise. The adoration and invocation are indicated in the first meditation. Begin by the golden bead, which symbolizes midnight.

Prayer Bead of the Year

Select a name of a God related to the sun.

With the prayer beads in your hands, take a golden bead between your thumb and forefinger, and declaim:

May the power of the sun illuminate all the levels of my being!

May the wheel of the sun turn, enlightening all the levels of my being!

May the sacred flame ignite the desire of the divine in all the levels of my being!

Continue by declaiming (or chanting) the name of the God on every bead. On the golden beads, you can either also pronounce the name of the God or the first sentence of the previous declamation.

INDIVIDUAL RITUAL
Tools
Consider the explanations provided for the lunar Goddess and do the same here.

Besides the tools needed, take the first solar prayer beads (of the day), and, if you can, a lunar incense and oil.

Opening
Follow the "Ritual of the Wheel of the Year" until the meditation period.

Take time to relax and breathe.

Solar Invocation

1. Use of the first prayer beads (daily cycle: twenty-four beads/four series of six/four separating golden beads)

Take your prayer beads in your right hand and the incense in your left.

Go to the east of the circle, facing east.

Raise your censer in this direction. Your thumb and forefinger are in contact with the first golden bead beginning the series of the day. Declaim the sunrise adoration provided in the previous meditation part.

Raise the censer for each pronunciation of the six following beads:

Heru-Khuti Khepera, hail unto thee!

When this is done, bow your head a few seconds in silence.

Then go south, west, and north, proceeding in the same way with the invocations provided in the previous meditation part.

When you are back to the east, raise once again your censer and declaim the last hymn beginning by "Hail unto thee, O Amon-Ra, the sacred falcon who delights…"

Come back in front of your altar and replace the censer.

It is good to have a period of meditation before closing the circle.

2. Use of the second prayer beads (zodiac cycle: forty-eight beads/twelve series of three/twelve separating golden beads)

Take your prayer beads in your right hand and the incense in your left.

Go to the east of the circle, facing east.

Raise your censer in this direction. Your thumb and forefinger are in contact with the first golden bead beginning the series of the day. Declaim the sunrise adoration provided in the previous meditation part.

Begin a clockwise circumambulation while declaiming (or chanting) the name of the God on every bead, including the golden beads.

Depending on what you usually do, it is possible to perform three circumambulations. In this case you will declaim three times the full prayer beads. It is not necessary to repeat the first invocation.

Two-person Ritual

One will be the Priest and the other one will be the Priestess.

Organization of the Place

Proceed in the same way you did for the ritual for the couple in the wheel of the year.

This ritual for the couple is performed during the meditation part. In this ritual work, one will be the receiver and the other one will perform the work. It doesn't matter who will be the receiver; however, it is a good idea to switch the roles.

1. Use of the first prayer beads of daily solar cycle

The receiver sits on a chair, facing east. The chair is not too close to the altar in order to allow the one performing the ritual to easily walk around.

For the sake of this example, I will suppose that the Priestess is the receiver and the Priest the one who performs the ritual. Remember that this is not a definitive rule.

Once the Priestess is seated, she closes her eyes and begins to breathe deeply and slowly. She relaxes.

The Priest stands in front of the altar, facing east.

The Priest opens his arms, breathes in silence, and declaims the following invocation:

I searched in the sky, I dug in the horizon, and I travelled the Earth in all directions to find the legacy of my elders.

I know all the secrets of creation, and the place where stands the crew of Ra's sacred bark.

I know the rebirths of Ra and his transformations in the deep waters.

I know the one who is in the bark of the day and in the bark of the night.

O Amon Ra, Master of the Horizon, gather your scattered limbs, and from the deepest darkness hear the praises of the crew of your bark and of the worshippers.

O Amon Ra, awake! You are the victorious One piloting the bark that carries light to the world.

O Amon Ra, arise, foster justice and destroy iniquity.

The Priest turns clockwise to face the Priestess.

With his prayer beads in his left hand, the Priest takes the first golden bead beginning the series of the day between his thumb and forefinger. He puts the palm of his right hand in contact with the head of the Priestess. Then he declaims the sunrise adoration while visualizing the God coming into him:

Hail unto thee, Khepera, in thy rising!

Hail unto thee, Heru-Khuti Khepera, creator of thine own manifestation!

When thou art in the bark of the morning, the winds rejoice thy heart.

At the limits of day, thy beauty is before me, O living Lord, and my soul proclaims that thou art my lord forever.

Hail unto thee, Khepera, in thy rising!

Heru-Khuti Khepera, hail unto thee!

One time on each of the six following beads, while visualizing a bright sunlight growing in the auras of the Priestess, the Priest declaims:

Heru-Khuti Khepera!

The Priest moves to the south of the Priestess and again puts his right hand on her head.

He takes the second golden bead beginning the second series of the day between his fingers and declaims the noon adoration:

Hail unto thee, Amon Ra, on this resplendent day!

Hail unto thee, Heru-Khuti Ra, Master of the Gods!

When thou art in thy bark above the skies, thy spreading golden light rejoices thy heart.

At the zenith of the day, thy beauty is without parallel, O living Lord, and my soul proclaims that thou art my lord forever.

Hail unto thee, Amon Ra, on this resplendent day!

Heru-Khuti Amon Ra, hail unto thee!

Visualizing the same light as he did in the east, he processes in the same way and declaims one time on each of the six following beads:

Heru-Khuti Amon Ra!

The Priest moves to the west of the Priestess and again puts his right hand on her head.

He takes the third golden bead beginning the second series of the day between his fingers and declaims the sunset adoration:

Hail unto thee, Temu, beautiful in thy setting!

Temu Heru-Khuti, thy rays are splendid to mine eyes!

When thou dost proceed in the bark of the evening, the wandering stars chant to thee, and the sentinel stars utter praises unto thee.

At the limits of day, thy beauty is before me, O living Lord, and my soul proclaims that thou art my Lord forever.

Hail unto thee, Temu, in thy setting!

Temu Heru-Khuti, hail unto thee!

Visualizing the same light as he did in the east, he processes in the same way and declaims one time on each of the six following beads:

Temu Heru-Khuti!

The Priest moves to the north of the Priestess and again puts his right hand on her head.

He takes the fourth golden bead beginning the second series of the day between his fingers and declaims the midnight adoration:

Hail unto thee, in thy hiding!

Thy rays have withdrawn from the world.

As thy bark proceeds pausely through the deep night, the wandering stars ever glorify thee. The sentinel stars utter praises unto thee.

In the deepest night, thou concealst thy beauty, O living Lord, and my soul proclaims that thou art my lord forever.

Hail unto thee, in thy hiding!

O Immortal God, hail unto thee!

Visualizing the same light he did in the east, he processes in the same way and declaims one time on each of the six following beads:

Ra!

The Priest moves to the east of the Priestess, replaces his prayer beads on the altar, again faces the Priestess, and again puts his hands on her head.

Then he declaims:

I invoke thee, Amon-Ra, sacred falcon who delights the land with beauty!

I invoke thee, Amon-Ra, thou who flies across the sky, traversing the earth and defeating the evil serpent!

I praise thee, O King of Eternity, thou who overturns his enemies and illumines the sanctuary of his adorers!

O Ra, may your light and power exalt ... *name of the Priestess* ...

O Ra, may your divine presence protect and illuminate the heart of ... *name of the Priestess* ...

So mote it be!

The Priest releases his arms and breathes.

After few minutes of meditation and relaxation, both Priest and Priestess continue the closing ritual of the wheel of the year.

GROUP RITUAL
Process

The group ritual uses the opening and closing of the "Ritual of the Wheel of the Year," using the prayer beads that represent the daily solar cycle (twenty-four beads separated in four series of six).

In the central part dedicated to the solar work, all the participants create a chain with their hands around the Priest and Priestess.

They are now repeating the invocations but they are declaiming the 24 (6x4) sacred names with the Priest.

When all the invocations are done, they release the chain.

Chapter 7

Druid Tradition

A wild land is definitely a mysterious place. Today, more than half the world's population lives in urban areas. It is well accepted that this number will continue to grow. In the east of Europe, it is harder to find wild places without any kind of human presence. The time of the large forests is quite over. This is different in other parts of the world, such as America and Australia, for example. However, the land hasn't completely lost its memory. Countries like France or Spain are full of archeological remains from the dawn of humanity.

I remember the countless times when, as a child, I explored the countryside of the southwest of France. In a single walk, I was able to enter a cave used by our prehistoric ancestors, see flint artifacts of this period on the ground, take a nap under a dolmen dating from the early Neolithic period (4000 to 3000 BCE), and touch stones from the Druidic and Roman periods. When you are young, this is at once fascinating and common. All these strata of history create a powerful, vivid, and heavy memory.

Druidism was a moment in history that was developed in the Gaulish and Celtic world. While the Roman world was expanding its presence all around the Mediterranean Sea and beyond, Druidism was still the religion of the land. It is interesting to note that the Gaulish and Celtic worlds were composed of various tribes. Each of them worshipped Gods and Goddesses, sometimes identical, sometimes different. It is not obvious that a united theology and philosophy existed at this time. Stories written in the Middle Ages were often written by people raised with a Christian background. That means monotheism and Christianity in particular were used as a reference to describe the ancient traditions and religions. It is not surprising, then, to discover Druidism depicted as a monotheist philosophy rooted on Trinitarian principles.

Neo-Druidism was born in the eighteenth century as a cultural movement which, through the following centuries, progressively became a religious movement often presented as a philosophy. This revival of a romantic vision of the ancient Druidic religion spread first in continental Europe and then progressively all over the world. Due to the absence at this time of any archeological discoveries regarding temples, Druids were seen as close to nature and possessors of a secret knowledge taught in an oral tradition. In the nineteenth and twentieth centuries, groups were progressively organized on a structure close to Freemasonry. People were organized in groups sometimes called a "clearing." Symbolic initiations were composed of three steps. Local groups were united in a larger organization with a Grand Druid. It was clearly identical to Freemasonry, with a Grand Master elected to represent the Masters of the Lodges, which compose the Grand Lodges.

This is not really surprising because for a long time, Druidism was a specific Masonic organization.

Progressively, Neo-Druidism spread from Freemasonry and eventually became a large and powerful religious movement.

During the twentieth century, several writers tried to discredit this revival of the ancient religion. It is true that the modern Druidic religion is often far from what it originally was. However, I must emphasize that the prefix "neo" is absolutely not pejorative. Most of the time, modern Druidism is an honest religious reconstruction built on texts that can be quite old. More often, I have met several Druids (female and male) who explained to me that their knowledge and lineage came from their family. Talking to, performing rituals with, and receiving teachings from them convinced me of the veracity of their affirmations. It is interesting to see that people claiming this sort of lineage were not in charge of large groups and were discreet. Signs and symbols were often connected to meeting initiates like them.

As you may know, France is a place where Druids and their religion flourished. As mentioned before, there are still people who claim to have received their initiation and tradition directly from their family. I was lucky enough to meet a woman Druid and a man Druid. Both occasionally attended modern Druidic groups, but remained free from any responsibilities to them. They knew the kind of heritage received in their family, and that was enough for them. They were Druids and that was the only thing that mattered, for them and me.

I remember going to a private Druidic ceremony in the forest. A Druid initiate was planning to show me how to use the energy of the ground to be harmonized with the divinities around us. Close to the meeting place, I saw an eagle flying above my head with a long, living snake in his claws. Even though I had lived in this region from my birth, it was the first time I had seen such a thing. The symbolic relation between this eagle and the ritual planned was obvious.

Druidism today has an interesting religious focus on nature. The celebrations are always performed outside and are intended to help you develop a balanced relation with Mother Nature. The principles are not so different from Wicca and can be easily connected. Let's say that usually Wicca focuses more on magick than Druidism does. It is also interesting to recall that one of my predecessors in the Aurum Solis, the previous Grand Master "Thomas Maughan," was a Grand Druid. The Order keeps this heritage alive.

When I was introduced into the Druidic mysteries, I never saw prayer beads. Invocations, prayers, and sacred words were used, but not as mantras repeated in sequence as we can do with the prayer beads. However, it is clear that prayer beads can be used profitably by anyone interested in the Druidic tradition. This beautiful, symbolic tool can be used in individual or group rituals. It is also a good way to internalize and memorize teachings from this tradition. If you already know Druidism, I encourage you to try out these prayer beads in your practices and rituals. If you don't know Druidism, I encourage you to use this tool as a first step in your discovery of this beautiful tradition.

Ritual of the Tribann

The Tribann[36] is a powerful symbol used in several groups of the modern Druidic movement. It was unknown in the ancient Celtic world, but was progressively adopted in modern times. Some Druids wear a white ribbon around the head with the Tribann embroidered on it and placed on the forehead. Sometimes a headdress is used instead of the ribbon with the Tribann positioned in the same place. This representation of three lines is the symbol of the three primeval sounds used by God to create the cosmos. These sacred vowels are O, I, and W. The latter is pronounced "ou." These letters are supposed to be the name of God itself. This is a Trinitarian representation of a celestial manifestation whose origin can be easily found in nature.

Perhaps you have been outside looking at the sky and it happens that the sun's rays pass through the clouds and create a kind of pyramid of light. Of course you cannot see the sun, which is hidden by the clouds, but you can see these rays (*bann*). This is exactly the material and spiritual representation of this beautiful symbol.

Druids also explain that the meaning of these three rays of light can be love-beauty (Karantez), knowledge-wisdom (Skiant), and truth (sometimes strength, Nertz). For others, they represent the male, female, and neutral. They can also be associated with the elements as follows: I, Water, Female | O, Fire, Male | W, Air, Neutral. The fourth element, Earth, is absent because it is obvious that you stand on the Earth looking at the

---

36. *Bann* means "ray" in Briton.

sky. These rays of light are also the symbol of the God Lugh (God of the light of the sun).

Description of the Prayer Beads

This set of prayer beads is composed of three strings of ten white beads. These strings are linked on one side to a golden ring.

Purpose

This is the origin of everything. Using these prayer beads to declaim the sacred vowels is a way to increase light in your aura. You progressively become like the Sun. Your physical and spiritual bodies receive this sun power, and their level of vibrations is accelerated. Health is increased in a well-balanced way.

Meditation

If you can, it is better to do this meditation outside and during the day. The presence of the sun is even better, but be careful if you decide to perform this meditation directly under the sun. Use a hat, sunglasses, and sunscreen. Sunrise is one of the best moments for such a meditation. Remember to face east.

Sit with your legs crossed in a position common to yoga and several Celtic Gods.

Opening

Take your prayer beads in your hands, close your eyes, and breathe regularly. Don't visualize anything. Just feel your respiration, the light on your body, the contact with the ground, the smell of the surrounding plants, etc.

After a few minutes, say:

May peace prevail in the East!
May peace prevail in the South!
May peace prevail in the West!
May peace prevail in the North!

With your prayer beads in your right hand, you will do the sacred sign of the Druidic cross.

Touch your forehead and say:

By the power of Belenus[37];

With the prayer beads, touch your belly, saying:

Teutates[38];

With the prayer beads, touch your left shoulder, saying:

Taranis;

With the prayer beads, touch your right shoulder, saying:

And Esus;

With the prayer beads, touch the center of your chest, saying:

---

37. Also named "Bel," or "Belenos."
38. Also named "Toutatis." Teutates, Hesus, and Taranis constitute a triad of Gaulish Gods that were worshipped by ancient Celtics.

Awen[39]!

Breathe for a few minutes in silence.

Then declaim the invocation to Belenus:

O Belenus, protector of the world, I bow before thee;

Bow your head for a few seconds. Then continue with the following text.

Protect me as I now invoke you;

Protect the wise and their books;

Protect all workers and their tools;

Protect my family and home from any harm or devilry;

Protect and inspire the writers and artists;

Inspire me in my life;

Grant me love, goodness, good health, and joy;

For this day and the days to come!

---

39. Pronunciation (from the Hebrew chart): aooain.

Main Meditation

1.Take the first bead of one of the strings of prayer beads between your thumb and forefinger and sing (or vibrate) the first sacred vowel: **"I."**

Continue to vibrate this sound on each bead of this string.

2. When this is done, declaim the prayer to Belenus again.

Proceed as you did for the first string with the second sacred vowel: **"O."**

3. Declaim the prayer to Belenus for the third time.

Proceed as you did for the second string with the third sacred vowel: **"W."**[40]

(If you have time and want to deepen your meditation, you can perform this cycle two more times in order to reach a number of three.)

Breathe in silence and after a few seconds, take the golden ring between your fingers and declaim the following prayer:

O God, grant me your support;

With your support, strength;

With strength, understanding;

With understanding, science;

With science, the knowledge of what is just;

---

40. Pronounce "ou."

With the knowledge of what is just, the power of loving it;

With the power of loving it, the love of all living things;

With the love of all living things, the love of God;

Of God and all Goodness!

You can conclude with a moment of silence, visualizing the light of the sun all around you, giving life to all levels of your being.

Individual Ritual
Tools

If possible, perform this ritual outside in a wild and silent place. You can also do this ritual indoors. If you are inside, you can hang a representation of the Tribann on the east wall.

It is best to make a ribbon from a white fabric (linen or cotton) and to paint (or embroider) the golden Tribann at the center of it.

If you have white clothes, you can wear them. If not, choose comfortable clothes and place the ribbon around your head in order to have the Tribann just in the center of your forehead.

Install a simple altar on a rock (or table). Put a white altar cloth on it. Place three candles on it in the shape of a triangle with its base toward the east and the apex toward you.

If you can drink wine, choose a white wine or mead. Pour the wine in one cup and put a second empty one on the altar for the libations.

Put a censer in the middle of the altar along with incense.

The circle around the place will be made with a white cord.

Opening

Casting the Circle

Light the three candles and the incense.

Take the censer and go to the east of the circle. Raise the censer and say:

May peace prevail in the East!

Go the south, facing this direction. Raise the censer and say:

May peace prevail in the South!

Go to the west, facing this direction. Raise the censer and say:

May peace prevail in the West!

Go the north, facing this direction. Raise the censer and say:

May peace prevail in the North!

Come back to the east, and circumambulate three times.

Come back to your altar, replace the censer, and take your prayer beads.

The Druidic Cross

As explained in the meditation, invoke on yourself the powers of Belenus, Teutates, Taranis, and Esus with the sacred sign of the Druidic cross.

Breathe for a few minutes in silence.

Invocation to Belenus

Declaim the invocation to Belenus:

O Belenus, protector of the world, I bow before thee;

Bow your head a few seconds. Then continue with the following text.

Protect me as I now invoke you;

Protect the wise and their books;

Protect all workers and their tools;

Protect our families and homes from any harm or devilry;

Protect and inspire the writers and artists;

Inspire us in our life;

Grant us love, goodness, good health, and joy;

For this day and the days to come!

Prayer to the Ancestors

Open your arms and declaim:

> **Benevolent spirits and souls of my ancestors, accept my prayers and support!**
>
> **Help me, guide me, advise me, and I will build a better world for the good of everything!**

Invocation of the Light

You can choose to sit in the same position described in the meditation, kneel, or stand.

If needed, add more incense in order to get a perfumed smoke.

Proceed with your prayer beads as you did during the meditation with the pronunciations of the sacred vowels. You can choose between one cycle or three.

Breathe in silence and after a few seconds, take the golden ring between your fingers and declaim:

> **O divine Sun, I invoke thee!**
>
> **Grant me a good life, good health, and make me strong!**
>
> **Grant me a clear victory over evil by the power of science which provides knowledge, the power of Love which provides life, and the Moral power which provides courage.**

Grant me the three human privileges: the discernment of Good and Evil, the freedom of choice, and the power to do it.

Help me to accomplish my three daily duties: worship the Gods, not harm anyone, and be just to all living creatures.

Help me to achieve my three goals: tame evil, exalt good, and achieve my destiny.

Help me to achieve the three main aspects of existence: Love, Truth, and Knowledge!

Closing

Stand up, replace the prayer beads on your altar, and take the cup in which you poured the mead. Raise the cup toward the sky and say:

By the power of OIW,

Trace with the cup the three rays of light of the Tribann from top to bottom, beginning with the left, then right, then central vertical. You will pronounce the vowels while you draw the line.

I ... *say your name* ... offer this sacred beverage to the Gods and Goddesses of this land.

Pour a part of the beverage on the ground if you are outside, or in the empty cup if you are inside.

May your presence be always a source of good for all the creatures living in your country.

So mote it be!

Drink the remaining part of the beverage and replace the cup. Open your arms and declaim the following prayer:

O God, grant me your support;

With your support, strength;

With strength, understanding;

With understanding, science;

With science, the knowledge of what is just;

With the knowledge of what is just, the power of loving it;

With the power of loving it, the love of all living things;

With the love of all living things, the love of God;

Of God and all Goodness!

Meditate in silence for a while, visualizing sunlight all around you providing life, strength, and health.

Put out the candles and say:

I began this ceremony in peace; may peace remain with me now and in the days to come!

Two-person Ritual
Organization of the Place and Process

The process is quite the same for a couple as it is for individual practice. The place is prepared in the same way, but you will draw a larger circle in order to allow you and your partner to walk easily. I will use the words Priest and Priestess to indicate their ritual functions.

Opening

Casting the Circle

The Priest lights the three candles and the Priestess lights the incense.

The Priestess takes the censer and goes to the east of the circle. She raises the censer and says:

May peace prevail in the East!

She proceeds to the south, west, and north, declaiming the same invocation adapted to the directions.

When she comes back to the east, the Priest joins her and they circumambulate three times.

They come back to the altar. She replaces the censer.

One of the couple will now be the receiver and the other will perform the work for him (or her). For clarity of the explanation, I will assume that the Priestess is the receiver and the Priest the officiant. Of course, the function can be changed for the good of the partners.

The receiver will sit in front of the altar, facing east. Keep at least three feet of distance between the altar and the receiver in order for the other partner to circumambulate easily around her.

When the Priestess is ready and relaxed, the Priest adds incense to the censer and goes to the east of the receiver. He faces her, raises the censer in her direction, and says:

From the East, I proclaim that peace must prevail in all the levels of your being!

The Priest proceeds in the same way in the south, west, and north.

He replaces the censer on the altar.

The Druidic Cross

The Priest places his prayer beads on his right hand, with the ring placed around the middle finger, and the three strings arranged on the top of the hand.

He puts his left hand on the top of the head of the Priestess.

With the tips of the fingers of his right hand, he will touch her forehead saying:

By the power of Belenus;

Touch the place of her belly, saying:

Teutates;

Touch her left shoulder, saying:

Taranis;

Touch her right shoulder, saying:

And Esus;

Touch the center of her chest, saying:

Awen!

The Priest replaces his prayer beads on the altar.

Invocation to Belenus

The Priest faces the Priestess and places the palms of his hands on the left and right sides of her head.

He declaims the invocation to Belenus:

O Belenus, protector of the world, hear my voice;

Protect ... *say the name of the receiver ...* **as I now invoke you;**

Protect the wise and their books;

Protect all workers and their tools;

Protect our families and homes from any harm or devilry;

Protect and inspire the writers and artists;

Inspire us in our life;

Grant us love, goodness, good health, and joy;

For this day and the days to come!

Prayer to the Ancestors

Keeping the same position, he declaims:

Benevolent spirits and souls of our ancestors, accept our prayers and support!

Help us, guide us, advise us, and we will build a better world for the good of everything!

Invocation of the Light

The Priest removes his hands, takes the anointing oil, and with his right thumb, draws the symbol of the Tribann on the forehead of the Priestess.

While drawing the first line (left) he pronounces one time the vowel "**I**."

The second line (right side) of the Tribann is associated with the sacred vowel "**O**."

During the drawing of the third line (central and vertical), he vibrates the vowel "**W**."

The Priest replaces the oil and takes the prayer beads in his left hand.

He directs the palm of his right hand toward the forehead of the receiver. He takes the first bead of one the strings of the prayer beads between his thumb and forefinger and sings (or vibrates) the sacred vowel "**I**."

The priest continues to vibrate this sound on each bead of this string.

When this is done, the Priest declaims:

O Belenus, protector of the world,

Inspire us in our life;

Grant us love, goodness, good health, and joy;

For this day and the days to come!

Then he proceeds as he did for the first string with the ten pronunciations of the second sacred vowel, "**O**."

When this done, he declaims for the third time the prayer to Belenus indicated above.

He proceeds as he did for the second string with the third sacred vowel, "**W**."

The Priest places the prayer beads on the right hand as he did before. He puts both hands above the head of the Priestess and declaims:

O divine Sun, I invoke thee!

Grant ... *say the name of the receiver* ... a good life, good health, and make her strong!

Grant her a clear victory over evil by the power of science which provides knowledge, the power of Love which provides life, and the Moral power which provides courage.

Grant her the three human privileges: the discernment of Good and Evil, the freedom of choice, and the power to do it.

Help her to accomplish her three daily duties: worship the Gods, not harm anyone, and be just to all living creatures.

Help her to achieve her three goals: tame evil, exalt good, and achieve her destiny.

Help her to achieve the three main aspects of existence: Love, Truth, and Knowledge!

Closing
The Priest replaces the prayer beads on the altar and says:

... *name of the receiver* ... arise!

The Priest takes the cup into which he poured the mead. He raises the cup toward the sky and says:

By the power of OIW,

The Priest draws with the cup the three rays of light of the Tribann from top to bottom, beginning with the left, then right, then central vertical. The Priest pronounces the vowels at the same time.

I ... *say your name* **... offer this sacred beverage to the Gods and Goddesses of this land.**

The Priest pours a part of the beverage on the ground if he is outside, or in the empty cup if he is inside.

May your presence be always a source of good for all the creatures living in your country.

So mote it be!

He gives the cup to the Priestess, who drinks part of the beverage.

The Priest drinks the remaining part of the beverage and replaces the cup.

The Priest and Priestess open their arms and declaim together the following prayer:

O God, grant me your support;

With your support, strength;

With strength, understanding;

With understanding, science;

With science, the knowledge of what is just;

With the knowledge of what is just, the power of loving it;

With the power of loving it, the love of all living things;

With the love of all living things, the love of God;

Of God and all Goodness!

They visualize the light of the sun all around them providing life, strength, and health.

The Priest puts out the candles and says:

I began this ceremony in peace; may peace remain with me now and in the days to come!

GROUP RITUAL

The process is the same as for the couple practice. Remember that the participants must remain inside the circle at all times. A few adaptations are necessary and they are explained below. One in the group will be chosen to be the receiver.

Opening

Casting the Circle

The process is the same except for the circumambulation.

Here, all the participants will make a chain with their hands. The altar must be the center of this chain. When the chain is established, all do three circumambulations, keeping their hands linked. At the end of these three circumambulations, the chain is released.

The Druidic Cross

When the Priest (or the one chosen for that) performs the Druidic Cross on the receiver, all move around the receiver and direct their hands toward her. Everyone should have his prayer beads placed on his hands in the same way the Priest did. They do not repeat the words declaimed by the Priest.

Invocation to Belenus

All direct their hands toward the receiver and declaim the invocation at the same time as the Priest.

Prayer to the Ancestors

All declaim the prayer.

Invocation of the Light

All pronounce the sacred vowels. The Priest is the only one who declaims the short invocation to Belenus.

When the Priest places both of his hands above the head of the Priestess and declaims the invocation to the sun, all pronounce the same text at the same time.

Closing

When the receiver drinks part of the beverage, the cup circulates around the circle and all the participants drink a little of it.

Then all declaim together the final prayer to God.

Ritual of the Celtic Cross

The Celtic cross is an old and beautiful symbol. It is often decorated with intertwining lines. We see such crosses in several places in the Celtic world. Several studies about its origin have been published, but the origin of this cross remains a mix of history and myth. There are also countless pieces of archaeological evidence of the long history of this representation. According to historians, the connection between the Celtic cross and Christianity is obvious. Even if the Celtic cross with four equal arms can be symbolically disconnected from the Christian religion, it is similar to the Christian cross, with a circle around the central point.

Nevertheless, the modern Druidic groups reclaimed this symbol and developed strong connections between it and similar Pagan representations. This is not the place to discuss the legitimacy of such symbolic development. It comes from people who were eager to reactivate the Druidic path and it gains its place in the history of the tradition.

Prior to focusing on these prayer beads and their practice, it is interesting to give you a few insights on this cross's symbolism. To be able to go further, you must consider its basic structure. The latter is surrounded by three circles, as you can see on the representation associated with this text.

Several archeological discoveries show us a diagram called the "triple surrounding walls." It has been discovered engraved in stones dating back to the Celtic period. This simple and mysterious representation can even be found all over the world. This is really an archetypal representation and the similarity with the Celtic cross can easily be noticed.

In the "Druidic triads,"[41] several paragraphs speak about the three levels of existence, which can be related to this specific cross:

"There are three circles in the Universal Life, in the world, which are: The empty circle (Ceugant) where no being but God can exist. Only manifestations of God can cross it and no living or dead creatures can access it. The circle of fate (Abred) is the place where all new existence comes from death. This is the circle of migrations that all living creatures must cross to reach the circle of ecstasy in knowledge (Gwynfyd) where all living beings come from life. This is the white world that Humans must reach after their transmigrations."

These three circles symbolize the movement of the souls. At first, they are lost in the chaos of Ceugant. Then they come to birth in Abred to experience the material world. From the world in which we live, we have two possibilities: ascend to the divine and reach the center of the cross (Gwynfyd) or be dragged into this life without any spiritual perspective. The consequence will be a return to the outer circle to come back another time, in another life.

As these correspondences between the three (or four) worlds have been a late construction associated with the cross, all explanations are not the same everywhere. There are, for example, a few differences between the respective positions of the

---

41. The full text of the triads can be found on my website at: www.debiasi. org.

worlds. Sometimes the smallest circle in the center is called An-nwn, sometimes Gwynfyd. The latter can also be found as an intermediary world located between Ceugant (out of the largest circle) and Abred.

It is not my goal in this book to say who is right and who is wrong. On the other hand, it is good to see what the common ground is. I will explain to you a way to use this cosmogony. If you already are practicing a Druidic path, the adaptation of this ritual to your system will be easy.

Abred is always explained as the intermediary world, the place of the transmigrations of the soul. There are three circles of existence and the soul is ascending to the divine level called Gwynfyd.

What is important here is the movement of the soul. The fact that this movement is symbolically represented from the exterior of the cross to its center or the opposite doesn't really matter. You only have to choose a direction and build your meditation on it.

The Druidic cross, also called Cross, has always been the second main symbol of modern Druidism with the Tribann.

One of the founders of Druidism, Paul Bouchet, revealed a beautiful way to represent the Druidic cross with sacred plants. Here is the description of it, from my personal and private archives:

"The outer circle (81), Ceugant, is shown as a garland of 37 oak leaves, each one having 7 veins and 11 oak nuts.

"The intermediary circle (27), Abred, is shown as a garland of mistletoe of 12 groups of 2 leaves and 9 white grains.

"The central circle (9), Gwynfyd, is composed of eight ears of wheat. Each one has 11 grains."

This representation succeeds in being beautiful, suggestive, and highly symbolic, all at the same time. There are various ways to use it. In this practice it will be used as a way to experiment with the triple surrounding walls and follow the travel of the soul. In the next ritual, it will help us connect to nature.

Purpose

This practice helps you to raise your consciousness and increase the vibrations of your spiritual body. There is an interesting side effect if you practice this ritual (or meditation) in the evening or night. Your dreams will be affected by this ritual work and you will learn more about the Druidic tradition and the root of the Western tradition.

Description of the Prayer Beads

This set of prayer beads is composed of eighty-one green beads, grouped in nine series of nine beads. These series are also separated in three larger groups that can been made with beads of three different greens: a) one series of nine beads (total of nine); b) two series of nine beads (total of eighteen); c) six series of nine beads (total of fifty-four). There are two kinds of separating beads. One separates the series a, b, and c, and the other separates the series of nine beads. A pendant representing the Druidic cross can be associated with these prayer beads.

Meditation

You can do this meditation either inside or outside. Usually your location doesn't affect the results of this inner practice.

As for the previous ritual of this chapter, sunrise is one of the best moments. Remember to face east.

Sit with your legs crossed in a position common to yoga and several Celtic Gods. You can also sit on a chair if this suits you more.

Opening

Take your prayer beads in your hands, close your eyes, and breathe regularly. Don't visualize anything. Just feel your respiration, and if you are outside, feel the light on your body, the contact with the ground, the smell of the surrounding plants, etc.

After a few minutes, say:

May peace prevail in the East!

May peace prevail in the South!

May peace prevail in the West!

May peace prevail in the North!

Take the first separating bead that introduces the six groups of nine beads.

With your prayer beads in your right hand and your thumb and forefinger on the separating bead, you will do the sacred sign of the Druidic cross as follows:

Say:

O God, I invoke you!

Touch your forehead, and say:

Grant me your support and your strength!

With the prayer beads, touch your belly, saying:

Grant me the understanding of the universe and its beings!

With the prayer beads, touch your left shoulder, saying:

Grant me the knowledge of what is just!

With the prayer beads, touch your right shoulder, saying:

Grant me the power of loving what is just!

With the prayer beads, touch the center of your chest, saying:

Grant me the love of all living things and the divine!

Nod your head and say:

So mote it be!

Main Meditation

Breathe in silence for a few minutes. Move your fingers onto the first bead of the first of the six series of nine beads.

On each bead, say:

I move forward on the path of Ceugant!

On each separating bead, repeat the Druidic cross as described before.

When you have finished the six series of nine beads, perform three times the invocation of the Druidic cross on the separating bead.

Breathe in silence for a few minutes. Move your fingers onto the first bead of the first of the two series of nine beads.

On each bead, say:

I move forward on the path of Abred!

On each separating bead, repeat the Druidic cross as described before.

When you have finished the two series of nine beads, perform three times the invocation of the Druidic cross on the separating bead.

Breathe in silence for a few minutes. Move your fingers onto the first bead of the last series of nine beads.

On each bead, say:

I move forward on the path of Gwynfyd!

When you have finished this unique series of nine beads, perform three times the invocation of the Druidic cross on the separating bead.

You can conclude with a moment of silence, visualizing a clear light surrounding you and giving life to all levels of your being.

Individual Ritual
Tools

You can perform this ritual either indoors or outdoors. If you are inside, you can hang a representation of the Druidic cross on the east wall.

If you have white clothes, you can wear them. If not, choose comfortable clothes.

Install a simple altar, like a table, at the center of your room. Put a white altar cloth on the top of it. In the center of this altar, place another representation of the Druidic cross and one candle on each of its branches, for a total of four candles.[42]

Put a censer on the left of the cross and your prayer beads on the right.

If the space allows you to do so, place on the floor three concentric circles made with a white cord. They represent the three circles of existence of the Druidic cross.

Opening

Casting the Circle

Stand at the west of the altar, facing east.

Light the four candles as described below.

When lighting the candle of the East, say:

May peace prevail in the East!

When lighting the candle of the West, say:

May peace prevail in the West!

---

42. See a representation of the altar on my website: www.debiasi.org.

When lighting the candle of the North, say:

May peace prevail in the North!

When lighting the candle of the South, say:

May peace prevail in the South!

Breathe in silence for a few minutes.

Invocation to Belenus
Declaim the invocation to Belenus:

O Belenus, protector of the world, I bow before thee;

Bow your head for a few seconds. Then continue with the following text:

Protect me as I now invoke you;

Protect the wise and their books;

Protect all workers and their tools;

Protect my family and home from any harm or devilry;

Protect and inspire the writers and artists;

Inspire me in my life;

Grant me love, goodness, good health, and joy;

For this day and the days to come!

Prayer to the Ancestors

Open your arms and declaim:

Benevolent spirits and souls of my ancestors, accept my prayers and support!

Help me, guide me, advise me, and I will build a better world for the good of everything!

Path of the Soul

Ceugant

Light the incense. Take the censer in your left hand and your prayer beads in your right hand.

With the incense burning, go outside the outer circle of cord. You are symbolically standing in the world of Ceugant.

Stand at the west of this circle, facing north. Then begin to turn clockwise around the cord. You must perform six circumambulations. During each one, use the first series of beads and declaim on each bead the words:

I move forward on the path of Ceugant!

You must be back at the west of the circle at the end of the series. You must stop, face east, and perform the Druidic cross as described before on the separating bead.

When the Druidic cross has been achieved, face north again and continue the circumambulations.

When the six circumambulations have been performed, stop as you did before at the west of the circle, face east, and do three times the invocation of the Druidic cross on the separating bead.

Abred

Step over the cord to enter the circle of Abred and at the same time, say:

With the help of the divine, I enter the world of Abred.

Face north and perform two circumambulations clockwise as you did for the previous circle.

During each one, use the series of beads and declaim on each bead the words:

I move forward on the path of Abred!

Stop as you did previously for the separating bead and the Druidic cross.

When the two circumambulations have been performed, stop as you did before at the west of the circle, face east, and do the invocation of the Druidic cross three more times.

Gwynfyd

Step over the cord to enter the circle of Gwynfyd and at the same time, say:

With the help of the divine, I enter the world of Gwynfyd.

Face north and perform one circumambulation clockwise as you did for the previous circle.

Use the series of beads and declaim on each bead the words:

I move forward on the path of Gwynfyd!

Stop as you did previously for the separating bead in front of your altar, facing east. Replace the censer on the altar.

Perform the invocation of the Druidic cross four times.

With your prayer beads still in your hands, raise your arm in front of you and draw with your forefinger a straight vertical line, at the same time singing the sacred vowel **"I."**

Raise your arm in front of you again and draw with your forefinger an inclined line on the left of the vertical line, at the same time singing the sacred vowel **"O."**

Raise your arm in front of you again and draw with your forefinger an inclined line on the right of the vertical line, at the same time singing the sacred vowel **"W."**[43]

Replace your prayer beads on the altar and sit for a silent meditation.

When you feel the moment is right, stand up and proceed to the closing of the ritual.

Closing

Open your arms and declaim the following prayer:

---

43. Pronounce "ou."

O divine Sun, I invoke thee!

Grant me a good life, a good health, and make me strong!

Grant me a clear victory over evil by the power of science which provides knowledge, the power of Love which provides life, and the Moral power which provides courage.

Grant me the three human privileges: the discernment of Good and Evil, the freedom of choice, and the power to do it.

Help me to accomplish my three daily duties: worship the Gods, not harm anyone, and be just to all living creatures.

Help me to achieve my three goals: tame evil, exalt good, and achieve my destiny.

Help me to achieve the three main aspects of existence: Love, Truth, and Knowledge!

Pause silently, visualizing the sunlight all around you providing life, strength, and health.

Put out the candles and say:

I began this ceremony in peace; may peace remain with me now and in the days to come!

Two-person Ritual
Tools and Process

You can use the same tools (add a specific oil or olive oil) as for the individual ritual, but the position of the altar is different.

For this two-person ritual, place the altar in the east of the room and not in the center of the circles as for the individual ritual.

In the center of the circles, place a chair for the receiver, facing east. Place four candles in the four directions on the floor and around the chair.

At the beginning of the ritual, the receiver sits on the chair and relaxes. During the process, he must remain calm, thinking only about his breathing. He should keep his mind open, welcoming any feelings, pictures, etc.

This two-person ritual follows essentially the same structure as the individual ritual. The differences are indicated in the explanation below.

Opening

Casting the Circle

Stand at the west of the altar, facing east.

Light the four candles as described in the previous rituals.

When lighting the candle of the East, say:

May peace prevail in the East!

When lighting the candle of the West, say:

May peace prevail in the West!

When lighting the candle of the North, say:

May peace prevail in the North!

When lighting the candle of the South, say:

May peace prevail in the South!

Breathe in silence for a few minutes.

Turn to face west and light the candle on the floor (east of the receiver). For each candle, use the same words you declaimed for the altar. Continue to light the other candles in the following sequence: south, west, and north.

Invocation to Belenus

Face the receiver and extend your hands toward his head.

Declaim the invocation to Belenus:

O Belenus, protector of the world, we invoke you;

Protect ... *name the receiver* ... as I now invoke you;

Protect the wise and their books;

Protect all workers and their tools;

Protect his family and home from any harm or devilry;

Protect and inspire the writers and artists;

Inspire him in his life;

Grant him love, goodness, good health, and joy;

For this day and the days to come!

Prayer to the Ancestors

Keeping your arms open and your hands toward the receiver, declaim:

Benevolent spirits and souls of the ancestors of ... *name the receiver ...* **, accept my prayers and support!**

Help him, guide him, advise him, and he will build a better world for the good of everything!

Path of the Soul

Proceed with the circumambulations as you did for the individual ritual.

The only differences are the declamations you do for the different circles performed around the receiver. Here is the text you should use.

For Ceugant:

May ... *name the receiver ...* **move forward on the path of Ceugant!**

For Abred:

May ... *name the receiver* **... move forward on the path of Abred!**

For Gwynfyd:

May ... *name the receiver* **... move forward on the path of Gwynfyd!**

The Druidic cross after each circumambulation is performed toward the receiver instead of the one who accomplishes the ritual.

Replace the incense and your prayer beads on the altar. Take the oil and anoint the forehead of the receiver while drawing the three lines of the Tribann and singing the three vowels: "I—O—W."

Sit for a silent meditation.

When you feel the moment is right, stand up and proceed to the closing of the ritual.

Closing

Face east, open your arms, and declaim the following prayer:

O divine Sun, I invoke thee!

Grant me a good life, good health, and make me strong!

Grant me a clear victory over evil by the power of science which provides knowledge, the power of Love

which provides life, and the Moral power which provides courage.

Grant me the three human privileges: the discernment of Good and Evil, the freedom of choice, and the power to do it.

Help me to accomplish my three daily duties: worship the Gods, not harm anyone, and be just to all living creatures.

Help me to achieve my three goals: tame evil, exalt good, and achieve my destiny.

Help me to achieve the three main aspects of existence: Love, Truth, and Knowledge!

Pause silently, visualizing sunlight all around the receiver, providing life, strength, and health.

Put out the candles around the receiver and the altar. Then say:

We began this ceremony in peace; may peace remain with us now and the days to come!

GROUP RITUAL
Process

The group ritual will be performed in the same way as the two-person ritual. There are a few differences I must highlight now.

When the incense is burning, it will be placed on the altar instead of being carried in the circumambulation.

The participants are in a circle all around the receiver. They are following the indications of the director of the ritual. Each one has prayer beads in hand. It is important to perform the ritual in harmony and in a coordinated movement.

The director of ceremony is the only one who will anoint the forehead of the receiver. However, all the other parts and invocations are accomplished by all the participants.

Ritual of the Nemeton

In the previous ritual, I talked about the symbolism of the Celtic and Druidic cross. The ritual highlighted the concentric circles as a representation of the three worlds of the Celtic cosmology. As you might expect, this famous symbol is not limited to these three circles. The Druids gave us two main clues to go forward: the plants you saw on the Druidic representation and the wheel shape of the cross itself.

As you may imagine, Druidism is a living approach to nature. Symbolism is never far from what surrounds you when you are outside in the wild. I chose to name this ritual the Gaulish word *Nemeton*. This ancient word means "sacred grove, sanctuary." In Europe, the word *clearing* is also used for the location where the ritual takes place.

I performed this ritual for the first time in a deep forest in the southwest of France. Not all parts of the forest are equal or sacred. Energies in the forest are different depending on the place you are—the trees, the stones, etc. Nothing is intellectual. The symbols are natural, simple, and powerful. This illustrates the power of such rituals. There are no complex dogmas, no long and obscure formulas to learn. Of course, it is necessary to know how to open this mysterious and invisible door, the simple words to repeat and repeat until the spiritual presences agree to your request.

This is what you have to keep in mind in this ritual. You will use words, symbols, and writings. However, don't forget that what is essential is to open your mind with humility and strength. This is a strange mixture, but it constitutes one of the efficient passwords needed to access the Nemeton.

Purpose

This ritual helps you to contact the spirits of the forest and your ancestors. These connections allow you to balance your inner energies in an efficient way. You will be able to increase your perception of the invisible world and your intuition.

Another deep effect can be observed from time to time. The inner connection with the spirit of the forest is similar to a shamanic experience. Then, as a consequence, your future can be changed to reveal the most authentic version of your being. Consequently, superficial activities can be dropped to reveal what is really essential for you. When it happens, this is a real gift from the divine.

Description of the Prayer Beads

These prayer beads are composed of eight series of eight green beads separated by eight golden beads. A pendant representing the Druidic (or Celtic) cross can be associated with these prayer beads.

Symbolism

Druids consider the arms of the cross as a representation of the four directions. The eight directions are also linked to the eight celebrations of the year in the Pagan calendar: Samhain (October 31), Yule (December 21), Imbolc (February 2), Spring Equinox (March 21), Beltane (April 30), Midsummer (June 21), Lughnasadh (August 1), and Autumn Equinox (September 21).[44]

These important markers also correspond to specific moments of the year. Four of them are related to the movements of the year and there is nothing to change here; the four other dates were chosen arbitrarily. I suggest you use the specific dates linked to the lunar calendar:

Beltane: Second full moon following the Spring Equinox.

Lughnasadh: Fifth full moon.

Samhain: Eighth full moon.

Imbolc: Eleventh full moon.

Another important symbolism is linked to the trees. There are several stories telling which trees are sacred and to which moment of the year they are linked. It is also important to associate this tradition to this ritual.

Samhain: Holly

Winter Solstice: Yew

Imbolc: Fir tree

---

44. As you may know, some of these dates change every year. However, they remain very close to the dates I indicate here.

Spring Equinox: Elm

Beltane: Ash

Summer Solstice: Apple tree

Lughnasadh: Hazel tree

Autumn Equinox: Sweet Chestnut

Center of the cross: Oak

Tools

I will give you the indications that you can use for an outdoor ritual. If you cannot perform the ritual in a forest, do it in your backyard or inside, visualizing everything. I have to emphasize that of course, it is best to go outside.

The choice of place is important. As you cannot be sure to find the perfect spot with four or eight trees in the right place, I suggest you focus only on the search for the central tree. If you can find an oak, it is good to use that, or another kind of tree. In Nevada where I live, there is a mountain with very old trees called bristlecone pines. These trees are the oldest living trees on the planet. You can rarely touch trees that are more than 5,000 years old. Obviously, you can learn many things from being in contact with such trees.

It is important to create a representation of the wheel (Celtic cross) around the tree you choose. For that, you should use four posts or small planks of wood to mark the two axes of the cross. You can also use four stones, but then it is important to bury a small part of the stone. Nevertheless, it is best to use posts of wood in order to engrave the names of the four directions.

I explained in a previous ritual that writings used in a ritual are more than just words; they are a way to connect to a specific egregore and attract its power to the space in which you are working. As I am talking here about the Druidic tradition perpetuated by the Gallic, it is important to use writings as they usually did. It is common to say that Druids did not use writings. Consequently, it is sometimes told that writings were not used at all, but this is not the case. On the contrary, archaeologists have found several artifacts engraved with Gaulish characters.

We know that the Gaulish alphabet was slightly different according to the area using it. The one I use here is called Lepontic and it has been subsumed under Gaulish even if it comes from the southeast of France. The words of the four directions in Latin have been transcribed into Gaulish characters.[45] By carving (or painting) and using them, you will realize that their power is efficient and interesting to use.

Of course, you can do the same with four rocks by painting the characters on them. If you are performing the ritual inside, just put the rocks (or poles) in the four directions.

Another aspect is important in the installation of the place: the position of the poles.

When you are preparing the place, you have to determine the four directions, the central point being the central tree. Use a compass to find north and consequently the other directions. If you know how to find the lines of energy in the ground, here is how you should proceed. Walk from the central tree in direction to the north and count four lines. As the

---

45. You can find the four words you should use on my website: www. debiasi.org.

space between two lines is around six to seven feet, the point you are looking for is approximately twenty-five feet from the central tree. Find now the closest knot of energy on the right.[46] Stick the pole in the ground on this location, engravings facimg the central tree. Do the same if this is a stone.

If you don't know how to use dowsing to find the lines of energy, just walk in a northerly direction, feeling the energy of the place and stopping when your intuition tells you to do so.

Proceed in the same way for the three other directions. At the end of this process, your central tree will be surrounded by the four poles erected in the four directions.

This simple installation is a very powerful and efficient tool you can use to build your Nemeton.

The traditional way consists of adding garlands of evergreen plants on the poles. Feel free to do that or just add ribbons on each pole.

Close to the central tree, place a censer, oil (specific one or olive oil), and your prayer beads.

If you are working inside, I suggest installing a representation of the Druidic cross on the east wall.

These tools will be the same for the meditation and the following rituals.

Meditation

If you perform this meditation indoors, you may adapt the following explanations.

Go outside and find "your" tree. When you have found the right one, sit against the east side of the tree, facing this direction.

---

46. A diagram of this can be found on my website: www.debiasi.org.

Relax and breathe, feeling the tree against your back and opening all your senses to this place.

Choose the quietest moment of the day.

Opening
Proceed for the opening as you did in the first meditation of the ritual of the Tribann.

Main Meditation
On the first golden bead, declaim:

O Sun, I invoke you.

Touch your forehead and say:

May the shadows be dispersed by the bright rays of your glorious light.

Touch your belly and say:

Deliver my soul from the darkness of my body.

Touch your left shoulder and say:

Give me health,

Touch your right shoulder and say:

strength,

Touch the center of your chest and say:

and success!

Bend your head in silence for a few seconds.
(The process must be the same for each golden bead.)
Begin the invocations on the first series of eight beads (one invocation on each bead for a total of eight by series).
1st series:

Spirits and Divine Powers of the East, I call upon you!

Balance all the parts of my being!

Give me health, strength, and success!

Continue the seven following series with the same words except the direction you have to change as indicated below:

2nd series: northeast

3rd series: north

4th series: northwest

5th series: west

6th series: southwest

7th series: south

8th series: southeast

Don't forget to proceed with the golden beads as described before.

When all the prayer beads have been achieved, say:

Temple worshipped by spirits and humans,

Glorious Tree,

Give me a part of your strength and wisdom.

Protect me and talk to the Gods about me!

Breathe in silence, open to the blessings received from the tree against which you sit.

When you think that the moment has come to end for this meditation, stand up, turn to face the tree, and kiss his bark with love and gratitude.

Individual Ritual

Proceed for the installation of the place as described in the previous part called "Tools." I recommend adding four stones in the four directions without posts: northeast, northwest, southwest, and southeast. You should use the same process that was used to place the posts.

Opening

Casting the Circle

Stand at the east of the tree, facing east. Take the oil and the incense and go to the post erected to the east. In front of it and facing this direction, raise your censer four times, saying once at the same time:

May peace prevail in the East!

Anoint the top of the post and say:

May the powers of the Earth and the sky coming from the East be manifested in this sacred place!

Come back to the central tree and raise your censer in its direction four times.

At the same time, say:

Temple worshipped by spirits and humans,

Glorious Tree,

Give me a part of your strength and wisdom.

Protect me and talk to the Gods about me!

Anoint the tree.

Go to the post erected to the north and proceed in the same way you just did for the east. In the declamations, simply change the names of the directions. Always come back to the central tree after invoking each direction.

When you are back to the east of the central tree, replace the censer and the oil. Breathe in silence for a few minutes.

Invocation to Belenus

Face east once again and declaim the invocation to Belenus:

O Belenus, protector of the world, I bow before thee;

Bow your head for a few seconds. Then continue with the following text:

Protect me as I now invoke you;

Protect the wise and their books;

Protect all workers and their tools;

Protect my family and home from any harm or devilry;

Protect and inspire the writers and artists;

Inspire me in my life;

Grant me love, goodness, good health, and joy;

For this day and the days to come!

Prayer to the Ancestors
Open your arms and declaim:

Benevolent spirits and souls of my ancestors, accept my prayers and support!

Help me, guide me, advise me, and I will build a better world for the good of everything!

Creation of the Nemeton

Take your prayer beads and go in front of the east post. With your fingers on the first golden bead, look toward the sky in the east and declaim:

O Sun, I invoke you in the East.

Touch your forehead and say:

May the shadows be dispersed by the bright rays of your glorious light.

Touch your belly and say:

Deliver my soul from the darkness of my body.

Touch your left shoulder and say:

Give me health,

Touch your right shoulder and say:

strength,

Touch the center of your chest and say:

and success!

Bend your head in silence for a few seconds.

(The process must be the same for each golden bead.)

Walk to the northeast as you declaim the invocation on the first series of eight beads (one invocation on each bead for a total of eight by series).

1st series:

Spirits and Divine Powers of this Nemeton, I call upon you!

Balance all the parts of my being!

Give me health, strength, and success!

When you are in front of the stone placed in the northeast, stop, face this direction and proceed as you did for the east, only changing the name of the direction.

Continue the seven following series with the same words except the change of direction as indicated below:

2nd series: from the northeast

3rd series: from the north

4th series: from the northwest

5th series: from the west

6th series: from the southwest

7th series: from the south

8th series: from the southeast

Don't forget to proceed with the golden beads as described before.

When the full set of prayer beads has been achieved, come back to the central tree and talk to him, saying:

Temple worshipped by spirits and humans,

Glorious Tree,

Give me a part of your strength and wisdom.

Protect me and talk to the Gods about me!

Perform three circumambulations clockwise around the tree. When you are back to the east of the tree, you must sit and meditate in order to receive the blessings from the tree and all the powers invoked in this sacred place.

Closing

When you think that the moment has come to end this ritual, stand up, turn to face the tree, and kiss his bark with love and gratitude.

Breathe in silence and after a few seconds, declaim:

O divine Sun, I invoke thee!

Grant me a good life, good health, and make me strong!

Grant me a clear victory over evil by the power of science which provides knowledge, the power of Love

**which provides life, and the Moral power which pro-
vides courage.**

**Grant me the three human privileges: the discernment
of Good and Evil, the freedom of choice, and the power
to do it.**

**Help me to accomplish my three daily duties: worship
the Gods, not harm anyone, and be just to all living
creatures.**

**Help me to achieve my three goals: tame evil, exalt
good, and achieve my destiny.**

**Help me to achieve the three main aspects of existence:
Love, Truth, and Knowledge!**

Remember to leave the place as you found it. "Leave no trace"
must be an absolute rule when you are performing activities
outside, ritual or not.

Two-person Ritual
Organization of the Place and Process

In this ritual, the receiver will sit comfortably against the tree.

Then the Magus will perform the ritual as it is described in
the individual ritual.

A few sections of the ritual must be adapted to the presence of the receiver as you can read below.

Opening

Casting the Circle

Stand at the east of the tree, facing east, and close to the receiver.

Take the oil and the incense and go to the post erected to the east. In front of it, raise your censer four times toward the east, at the same time saying:

May peace prevail in the East!

Anoint the top of the post and say:

May the powers of the Earth and the sky coming from the East be manifested in this sacred place!

Come back to the central tree and raise your censer toward it four times.

At the same time, say:

Temple worshipped by spirits and humans,

Glorious Tree,

Give to ... *name the receiver* **... a part of your strength and wisdom.**

Protect him and talk to the Gods about him!

Anoint the tree and the forehead of the receiver.

Go to the post erected to the north and proceed in the same way you just did for the east. Just change the names of the directions in the declamations. Always come back to the central tree after invoking each direction.

When you are back to the east of the central tree, replace the censer and the oil. Breathe for a few minutes in silence.

Invocation to Belenus
Face east once again and declaim the invocation to Belenus:

O Belenus, protector of the world, I bow before thee.

Bow your head for a few seconds. Then continue with the following text:

Protect ... *name the receiver* **... as I now invoke you;**

Protect the wise and their books;

Protect all workers and their tools;

Protect his family and home from any harm or devilry;

Protect and inspire the writers and artists;

Inspire ... *name the receiver* **... in his life;**

Grant him love, goodness, good health, and joy;

For this day and the days to come!

Prayer to the Ancestors

Open your arms and declaim:

> **Benevolent spirits and souls of my ancestors, accept my prayers and support!**
>
> **Help ... *name the receiver* ... , guide him, advise him, and he will build a better world for the good of everything!**

Creation of the Nemeton

Take your prayer beads and move one step forward toward the east. With your fingers on the first golden bead, look toward the sky in this direction and declaim:

> **O Sun, I invoke you in the East.**

Turn to face the receiver and touch his forehead, saying:

> **May the shadows be dispersed by the bright rays of your glorious light.**

Touch his belly and say:

> **Deliver his soul from the darkness of his body.**

Touch his left shoulder and say:

> **Give him health,**

Touch his right shoulder and say:

strength,

Touch the center of his chest and say:

and success!

Bend your head in silence for a few seconds.

(The process must be the same for each golden bead.)

Face the east again as you declaim the invocation on the first series of eight beads (one invocation on each bead for a total of eight by series).

1st series:

Spirits and Divine Powers of this Nemeton, I call upon you!

Balance all the parts of the being of ... *name the receiver* ... !

Give him health, strength, and success!

Turn left to face the northeast and proceed as you just did for the east.

Continue the following series with the same words except you change the directions as indicated below:

3rd series: from the north

4th series: from the northwest

5th series: from the west

6th series: from the southwest

7th series: from the south

8th series: from the southeast

When the complete series of prayer beads has been achieved, come back in front of the receiver, facing the central tree, and talk to him, saying:

Temple worshipped by spirits and humans,

Glorious Tree,

Give ... *name the receiver* ... a part of your strength and wisdom.

Protect him and talk to the Gods about him!

Perform three circumambulations clockwise around the tree. When you are back to the east of the tree, place your right hand on the top of the receiver's head and your left hand in contact with the tree.

Repeat three more times the previous invocation, "Temple worshipped ..."

Feel the energy of the tree you concentrate in the receiver.

After this sequence, you can sit to the west of the tree and meditate for a few minutes in order to receive its blessings and all the powers invoked in this sacred place.

Closing

When you think that the moment has come to end this ritual, stand up, ask the receiver to do the same, turn to face the tree, and kiss his bark with love and gratitude.

Breathe in silence and after a few seconds, both of you should declaim:

O divine Sun, I invoke thee!

Grant me a good life, good health, and make me strong!

Grant me a clear victory over evil by the power of science which provides knowledge, the power of Love which provides life, and the Moral power which provides courage.

Grant me the three human privileges: the discernment of Good and Evil, the freedom of choice, and the power to do it.

Help me to accomplish my three daily duties: worship the Gods, not harm anyone, and be just to all living creatures.

Help me to achieve my three goals: tame evil, exalt good, and achieve my destiny.

Help me to achieve the three main aspects of existence: Love, Truth, and Knowledge!

As you did in the individual ritual, remember to leave the place as you found it.

Group Ritual

The process is the same as the practice for a couple. A few adaptations are necessary, explained below. One in the group will be chosen to be the receiver.

Opening: Casting the Circle

The process is slightly different depending on the number of participants. If there are nine persons (the receiver plus eight participants), the eight directions should be assigned to each of them. If there are between five and nine, the four directions should be assigned to four different participants. If there are fewer than five, the celebrant performs the eight directions himself.

This ritual is the same as the two-person ritual, except for the circumambulation.

Here, all the participants will make a chain with their hands. The altar must be the center of this chain. When the chain is established, all do three circumambulations, keeping their hands linked. At the end of these three circumambulations, the chain is released.

Invocations to Belenus and Prayer to the Ancestors

All direct their hands toward the receiver and declaim the invocation at the same time as the celebrant.

Creation of the Nemeton

All are placed around the tree and the receiver. They will move all together, counterclockwise. They will stop eight times during this circumambulation. The position of the celebrant indicates the direction to be invoked. All declaim the invocation at the same time. Instead of touching the receiver during the prayer on the golden bead, all extend their arms, hands opened toward the central tree and the receiver.

At the end, all make a chain with their hands and make three clockwise circumambulations. The celebrant proceeds as for the two-person ritual. Meanwhile, all the participants touch the tree and maintain this position.

Closing

The process of the closing is the same as for the previous ritual. If the tree is too small to allow everyone to kiss the tree at the same time, they will do it by turns on the east side of the tree.

As you did in the individual and two-person ritual, remember to leave the place as you found it.

Conclusion

This book is an initiation into a special kind of magick using a wonderful tool called prayer beads. When you begin to use them regularly, you may never stop. This magical tool is an important key to the spiritual world.

It gives you the opportunity to master several psychic abilities that can be challenging to manage. Visualization, invocations, breathing, and gestures are all used in the rituals provided in this book.

I strongly recommend using these spiritual practices regularly. Remember to experiment with traditions you are not familiar with. This is always a great opportunity to learn more about yourself.

In magick the idea of a spiritual chain is important. With prayer beads this symbol becomes obvious and effective. I am confident that by using prayer beads you will be drawn to other magick chains that will bring you to other dimensions.

Blessed Be!

Appendix

Guidelines for Greek Pronunciation

Remember that you can find other pronunciations slightly different, as ancient Greek differed through the years and in the countries that used this language.

The fourth column gives you the codes used in this book to indicate the pronunciations of the words in Greek. They also can be found in audio on my personal website and in the app related to this book.

Capital/Small Greek letters	English Names	Pronunciations
A α	Alpha	"a" as in father
B β	Beta	"b" as in baby
Γ γ	Gamma	"g" as in guess
Δ δ	Delta	"d" as in dead
E ε	Epsilon	"e" as in set
Z ζ	Zeta	"dz" (also sd)
H η	Eta	"e" as in hair
Θ θ	Theta	"th" as in thought
I ι	Iota	"e" as in meet
K κ	Kappa	"k" as in kill
Λ λ	Lambda	"l" as in leap
M μ	Mu	"m" as in met
N ν	Nu	"n" as in net
Ξ ξ	Xi	"ks" as in axis
O o	Omicron	"o" as in hot
Π π	Pi	"p" as in past
P ρ	Rho	"r" (can be rolled as the "r" in Italian or Scottish)
Σ σ	Sigma	"s" as in lesson
T τ	Tau	"t" as in top
Y υ	Upsilon	"u" as in Créme Brûlé
Φ φ	Phi	"f" as in foot
X χ	Chi	"k" as in chorus (can be also pronounced as in Scottish loch)
Ψ ψ	Psi	"ps" as in lapse
Ω ω	Omega	"o" as in only

Phonetic used in this book	Milesian & Alexandrian values
a	1
b	2
g	3
d	4
ê	5
dz	7
ai	8
th	9
i	10
k	20
l	30
m	40
n	50
x	60
o	70
p	80
r	100
s	200
t	300
u	400
f	500
kh	600
ps	700
ô	800

Extra Letters used in the early times

Digamma	6
Qoppa	90
Sampi	900

Diphtongs

au	Alpha-upsilon	"ow" as in all**ow**	ow
eu	Epsilon-upsilon	"eu" as in b**e**lt	eu
ou	Omicron-upsilon	"oo" as in **too**	oo
ei	Epsilon-iota	"ei" as in fianc**ée**	ei
ai	Alpha-iota	"ai" as in h**igh**	aï
oi	Omicron-iota	"oi" as in b**oy**	oï
ui	Upsilon-iota	"wee" as in s**wee**t	wee
hu	Eta-upsilon	"eu" pronounced longer than eu	euu
ô	Accent on a vowel	Rough breathing	ho

Guidelines for Hebrew Pronunciation

As with ancient Greek, remember that you can find other pronunciations slightly different, as Hebrew has differed through the years and in the countries that have used this language.

The fourth column gives you the codes used in this book to indicate the pronunciations of the words in Hebrew.

Hebrew Letters/ Final Letters (several letters change according the associated vowels)	English Names	Sounds in the words
א	Alef	(silent)
ב	Bet	"b" as in **b**aby— "v" as in **v**ictory
ג	Gimel	"g" as in **gu**ess
ד	Dalet	"d" as in **d**ead
ה	He	"h" as in **h**elp— Sometimes silent
ו	Vav	"v" as in **v**ictory— "o" as in **o**ption— "oo" as in t**oo**
ז	Zayin	"z" as in **z**ero
ח	Het	"ch" pronounced as in Scottish lo**ch**
ט	Tet	"t" as in **t**op
י	Yod	"e" as in m**ee**t
כ/ך	Kaf/khaf	"k" as in **k**ill—"ch" pronounced as in Scottish lo**ch**
ל	Lamed	"l" as in **l**eap
מ/ם	Mem	"m" as in **m**et
נ/ן	Nun	"n" as in **n**et

Phonetic used in this book	Numeric value of Hebrew Letters	Pronunciation of the letters
Depending the vowel associated to it.	1	alaif
b-v	2	bait
g	3	gimail
d	4	dalait
h—not indicated if silent.	5	hai
v-o-oo	6	vav
z	7	zain
kh	8	khait
t	9	tait
i	10	iod
k-*kh*	20/500	kaf-*kh*af
l	30	lamaid
m	40/600	maim
n	50/700	noon

Hebrew Letters/ Final Letters (several letters change according the associated vowels)	English Names	Sounds in the words
ס	Samekh	"s" as in lesson
ע	Ayin	(silent)
פ/ ף	Pe/Fe	"p" as in past— "f" as in folder
צ/ ץ	Tsadi	"ts"
ק	Qof	"k" as in kilo
ר	Resh	"r" as in random
ש	Shin / Sin	"ch" as in chilly— "s" as in lesson
ת	Tav	"t" as in top
	El	combination between Hair and in Rebel
	e	as in Hair
	He	combination between "h" in Hat and "ai" Hair
		As in butter
		as in ban
		"ai" as in high
		"g" as in George

Phonetic used in this book	Numeric value of Hebrew Letters	Pronunciation of the letters
s	60	samekh
Depending the vowel associated to it.	70	ain
p-f	80/800	pai-fai
ts	90/900	tsadi
k	100	kof
r	200	raich
ch-s	200	chin-sin
t	400	tav
ail		
ai		
hai		
eu		
n		
aï		
g		

Vowels

They are indicated by the consonants Alef, He, Vav, Yod, and vowel points associated to various letters.

To Write the Author

If you wish to contact the author or would like more information about this book, please write to the author in care of Llewellyn Worldwide, and we will forward your request. Both the author and publisher appreciate hearing from you and learning of your enjoyment of this book and how it has helped you. Llewellyn Worldwide cannot guarantee that every letter written to the author can be answered, but all will be forwarded. Please write to:

Jean-Louis de Biasi
℅ Llewellyn Worldwide
2143 Wooddale Drive
Woodbury, MN 55125-2989

Please enclose a self-addressed stamped envelope for reply, or $1.00 to cover costs. If outside the U.S.A., enclose an international postal reply coupon.